MATT FALCUS

50 AIRLINERS
THAT CHANGED FLYING

MATT FALCUS

50 AIRLINERS
THAT CHANGED FLYING

First published in 2018

The History Press
The Mill, Brimscombe Port
Stroud, Gloucestershire, Gl 5 2q G
www.thehistorypress.co.uk

British library Cataloguing in Publication Data.
A catalogue record for this book is available from the British library.

ISBN 978-0-7509-8583-3

Typesetting and origination by The History Press
Printed in China

Cover Illustrations

Upper Front: Despite its technological advances, only two
airlines ever ordered Concorde aircraft. (Author's Collection)

Lower Front: The fuselage of the Constellation has a distinctive
shape, with a bulbous forward fuselage that tapers to a point at
the tail, and three vertical fins spread across a wide horizontal
stabiliser. (Author's Collection)

Back Left: Passengers enjoy the comfortable spacious interior
of the Stratoliner.

Back Right: The Benoist Type XIV was probably the first
aircraft to fly a scheduled passenger service.

Page 2: Sud Aviation Caravelle cockpit. (Author)

Page 4: As well as comfortable passenger cabins, the DC-3 was
used as a troop transport during the Second World War. (Author)

CONTENTS

ACKNOWLEDGEMENTS

The author would like to thank a few individuals for their help and support in producing this book. Jon Proctor, whose experience working in the airline industry and collection of images from those days is beyond compare. I'd like to thank my wife, Lucy, for her support in my aviation interests, and my parents for encouraging me to follow this interest from an early age. Finally, I'd like to thank Amy Rigg and all at The History Press for bringing this book to life.

ABOUT THE AUTHOR

Matt Falcus is a British aviation writer and author of a number of books. His interests in aviation started at a young age when watching aircraft from the viewing terraces at his local airport. In 2003, he began writing articles for consumer magazines such as *Airliner World* and *Aviation News*, and has written popular guides for enthusiasts both online and in print. He has also been interviewed on BBC Radio 4, Radio 5 Live, and collaborated with organisations such as British Airways, London City Airport and the Royal Air Force. Matt is also a private pilot.

INTRODUCTION

Sitting on board an Airbus A380, among more than 500 other passengers, it's difficult to imagine that little over 100 years ago flight was a new, experimental endeavour. Early pioneers saw its potential in delivering the mail much quicker, and the onset of war meant great advancements in aeroplanes because of their ability to be used for military purposes. Yet flying one or two passengers was a novelty in those early days.

It took a number of years before the commercial possibilities of flying passengers and making money doing so dawned on aircraft manufacturers. The early limitations of aircraft, in terms of how far they could fly and how many passengers they could carry, certainly restricted their impact to small, expensive endeavours by a few entrepreneurial pioneers.

The first few decades of flight were an experimental time, with aircraft built in small numbers and their reliability being something of an issue. Yet by the 1930s great strides were being made to produce machines capable of comfort, range, speed and reliability that could be mass produced and prove suitable for the needs of air carriers all over the world. It did not take long before it became possible to link greater distances, across oceans and continents, with greater numbers on board.

With flying remaining the reserve of the rich, aircraft were developed with on-board luxuries reminiscent of the hotels and clubs one might visit, and heavily inspired by sea and train travel. Early airliners included wicker chairs in elegant saloons, with washrooms and impeccably dressed waiters. As aircraft grew in size, passengers would still regularly dress up to take a flight even into the 1960s.

Yet with the economics needed to make air travel pay, the advancement in aircraft turned in the direction of size and reducing costs. Aircraft and their engines became efficient at transporting large numbers of people over great distances, at speed, whilst reducing the cost of operating. In doing so, air travel was brought to the masses. Many might argue that, in today's world of low-cost carriers and routes linking thousands of city pairs, it is more akin to taking a bus than a luxury train or ocean liner.

A busy scene of early piston airliners at New York La Guardia during the post-war boom in air travel, made possible by pioneering aircraft designers and manufacturers, and the airlines that saw the opportunity. (Jon Proctor Collection)

However, along the way many great leaps have taken place. Those early piston aircraft with open cockpits very quickly gave way to luxury airliners with sleeping berths, pressurised cabins and engines capable of flying at greater speed. These in turn gave way to the jet age, flying higher and further in comfort. Aircraft such as Concorde enabled travel at immense speed, while the Boeing 747 'jumbo jet' became the so-called 'queen of the skies'. Finally, today's ultra-efficient airliners are built of composite materials that give strength at a fraction of the weight, and offer complex technology and computerised systems.

Great superpowers of aircraft manufacturing were established early on and were responsible for many great leaps and advances in design and technology. In the early days Britain, France and Russia were years ahead. Yet America proved that aircraft could be made commercially viable and produced in great numbers, creating important companies such as Boeing, Douglas and Lockheed. Europe's response has been the collaborative Airbus, whilst aircraft manufacturing in post-Soviet Russia has always remained strong.

The luxurious cabin of an early Imperial Airways aircraft. (Author's collection)

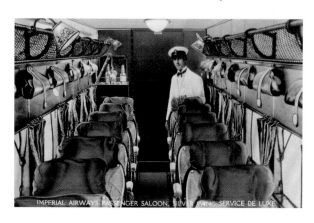

IMPERIAL AIRWAYS PASSENGER SALOON, SILVER WING SERVICE DE LUXE

The aircraft in this book have all played a major role in developing air travel in some important or pioneering way. Many are household names and have enjoyed a long-lasting impact on the way we travel; others have long been consigned to the history books and now can only be enjoyed in museums, yet must be remembered for their innovative contributions. Others are still flying thousands of passengers every day all around the world. Either way, these airliners will forever be responsible for shaping how we fly.

one

THE
EARLY
YEARS

On 17 December 1903, the world was changed forever when two pioneering brothers took to the skies for the first time in a heavier-than-air craft from a blustery beach, in front of a crowd of onlookers. Everything we know today about flight and aircraft would come from that moment, including its development for military and commercial purposes.

On that day, Wilbur and Orville Wright assembled their Wright Flyer aircraft, having aborted an earlier attempt a few days prior, on the beach at Kill Devil Hills, near Kitty Hawk, North Carolina. Using a rail as a runway, the pair tossed coins to decide who would make the first flight, so confident were they that their aircraft would indeed break the confines of gravity.

Launching into the wind, the first flight left the rail and travelled a distance of 120ft, with Wilbur at the controls. The distance was less than the wingspan of a modern large airliner, yet it was enough to propel the brothers into history.

The distance flown by the Wright Flyer was less than the wingspan of an Airbus A380. The only way a pilot could control the aircraft's direction was by lying on his stomach, facing forward, and manipulating levers with his hips to control the surfaces of the wings and tail plane.

Where it all began. The Wright Brothers and their Wright Flyer in North Carolina in December 1903.

Little is written about the aircraft itself, or what else happened that day. The Wright Flyer was influenced by the work the Wright brothers had carried out previously with gliders. It was a biplane built of spruce, with an engine designed specifically for the job to power two propellers.

For the remainder of that ground-breaking day the brothers took turns flying a further three times, each over a greater distance, until a heavy landing followed by a gust of wind damaged the aircraft; it would never fly again.

The Wright Flyer could by no means be described as an airliner, however it certainly changed flying and led to the development of passenger-carrying aircraft as we know them today. The design was not without flaws, and the most important thing to understand is that the results of testing this aircraft helped determine what would or would not work on future aircraft.

The Wright Flyer was stored in a barn for many years before its historical significance led to it being displayed in exhibitions around the world. On 17 December 1948, the forty-fifth anniversary of its only flights, it was put on display in the Smithsonian Institution in Washington DC, moving to its National Air and Space Gallery in 1976. It was fully restored in 1995.

Those familiar with the appearance of the large, sleek airliners that whisk passengers around the world at speed today might be forgiven for thinking this small flying boat was nothing more than an early experiment in flight. However, it was the aircraft that proved air travel could be profitable, albeit in a very short timescale.

Thomas Benoist was an automobile mogul, having made a fortune from the early years of cars. Following the invention of the heavier-than-air aeroplane by the Wright Brothers in 1903, Benoist had become firm in the belief that air travel would be the next great leap from the automobile and set about designing and building his own aircraft.

Alongside business partner Paul E. Frasler, the entrepreneur built the Benoist Type XIV in 1913 to operate for Frasler's new St Petersburg–Tampa Airboat Line in Florida. Widely regarded as the world's first scheduled airline, the first flight was on 1 January 1914. The new aircraft had the perfect opportunity to bridge the 18 miles between St Petersburg and Tampa that otherwise had to be navigated by lengthy road, rail or boat journeys.

The Benoist Type XIV itself was not remarkable in many ways, featuring a standard design of the time and operating from water. However, it could operate with a single passenger alongside the captain at a ticket price of $5 each way. The airline was able to pay its contract fees easily and make a profit, proving the viability of air travel on routes where it could offer such an advantage over ground or sea routes.

The route didn't last long due to political tensions; however, Benoist was spurred to build larger aircraft to cope with demand and opportunities were soon being realised around the country and the rest of the world to make air travel a commercial enterprise. The airline was born.

The Benoist Type XIV was likely the first aircraft to
fly a scheduled passenger service.

Not long after the invention of the aeroplane, its potential was realised around the world. Igor Sikorsky was a prolific aircraft designer in Russia who had been responsible for a succession of experimental fixed-wing aeroplanes, leading to his monstrous (at the time) Ruskii Vitiaz four-engine biplane, nicknamed 'Le Grande'.

Based on this design, Sikorsky went on to develop the Ilya Muromets class of aircraft, named after the Slavic folk hero. The principle behind the aircraft was to carry passengers and enter commercial service, serving the communities scattered throughout the Russian Empire, with luxuries built in that had rarely been seen before on board an aircraft, including a washroom and a spacious saloon for up to sixteen passengers.

The Ilya Muromets used four Argus AS I 100hp engines.

The initial S-22 model caused quite a stir and became the talk of Russia when it first flew in 1914. It had four Argus AS I engines delivering 100hp each, and would break all height records at the time by flying at 6,500ft (2,000m) above ground with a full payload of passengers. The range of the aircraft was 370 miles (600km).

The timing of the development of the Ilya Muromets coincided with the outbreak of the First World War. Despite its potential as a commercial airliner, the needs of the Russian military for a bomb-carrying aircraft far outweighed this, and all future development of the type shifted focus. It would be unrivalled in this new role and significantly help the war effort.

Nevertheless, the post-war Soviet commercial airliner industry indeed benefitted from the designs of the Ilya Muromets and other early Sikorsky aircraft, founding an industry that would see many important piston and jet airliners emerge to rival those being produced in the West.

During the First World War, Handley Page had developed the Type O aircraft, which was designed to carry mail and cargo but also passengers when needed. Following this, the British manufacturer's first dedicated foray into building dedicated commercial airliners came about with the Type W.

Three basic models emerged, the W.8, W.9 and W.10, first appearing at the 1919 Paris Air Show. They were loosely based on the Type O, but now included a larger, more spacious cabin capable of accommodating up to sixteen passengers, sat either side of a central gangway. By the time it entered airline service in October 1921, this had been reduced to twelve passengers, but now – for the first time ever – this aircraft featured a lavatory for passenger use.

Whilst the W.8 variants found uses on European routes, such as Brussels to Paris, the larger W.9 was not as successful and acted more as a stopgap to the W.10, of which four were built and operated for Imperial Airways from May 1926.

Their service life lasted only ten years, yet the legacy of on-board toilets lives on, for which Handley Page can be thanked as pioneers of such comforts.

Boarding an Imperial Airways Type W at Croydon
Airport. (Author's collection)

Handley Page Type W G-EBLE departing on a European scheduled flight. (Author's collection)

JUNKERS F13

All aircraft prior to 1919 had been built of wood, from the Wright Flyer to the first airliners of the era. This would continue to be the case for many designs over the coming decades, but German manufacturer Junkers had been experimenting in building aircraft with metal fuselages and wings.

The world's first all-metal airliner was the Junker F13, which first flew on 25 June 1919. As would become common with Junkers aircraft, the metal was corrugated to add strength. For the first time an airliner appeared without bracing wires across its wings, which gave it a sleek appearance that would hint at the future designs of airliners to come.

Around 350 Junkers F13s were built and they were available in a number of configurations. They could be fitted with skis, wheels or floats to operate in different environments, opening up air travel across Europe and elsewhere. Principal operators of this reliable aircraft included the new German national airline Lufthansa, and even Aeroflot in Russia.

One of the few surviving Junkers F13s. (Author)

The Junker F13 was the world's first all-metal airliner.
(Author)

50 AIRLINERS THAT CHANGED FLYING

Perhaps the most famous of the so-called tri-motor aircraft are the Junkers Ju 52 and the Ford Tri-Motor itself. However, neither were the first to adopt such an engine layout.

Unlike later aircraft, the Fokker F.VII was built of plywood and not metal. Initially it was to only use one engine, but Anthony Fokker heard rumours of the work Ford was doing on transport aircraft and ordered two additional engines added, this time under the wings, to supplement the one in the nose of the initial F.VIIa aircraft that had been built. The result was the F.VIIa/3m, which first flew in September 1925. It could carry twelve passengers in comfort in its enclosed cabin.

The most famous Fokker F.VII tri-motor was known as the *Southern Cross*. It was bought by aviator Charles Kingsford Smith in 1928, who undertook the first crossing of the Pacific by air. The flight took him from Oakland, California, to Brisbane, Australia, in eighty-three hours eleven minutes of flying time, with two stops en route, and he was greeted by 25,000 people. This particular aircraft is now preserved outside the passenger terminal at Brisbane Airport.

The Fokker F.VII saw commercial success with major airlines such as KLM, Sabena and TWA, before structural inadequacies saw early retirement in favour of the new all metal tri-motor aircraft and the ground-breaking Boeing 247 that appeared in the 1930s.

Above: The most famous Fokker F.VII tri-motor was known as the *Southern Cross*, which undertook the first crossing of the Pacific by air. (Author's collection)

Left: The Fokker F.VII saw commercial success with major airlines such as KLM, Sabena and TWA. (Author)

50 AIRLINERS THAT CHANGED FLYING

Like the Boeing 247 and Douglas DC-3, the Ford Tri-Motor is one of the most iconic American airliners of the era.

When it was built, the Ford 4-AT Tri-Motor was the largest airliner ever to have flown. This was in 1926, after the Ford Motor Company acquired Stout Metal, which had already developed a mail-carrying plane known as the 2-AT. The result was an all-metal aircraft with three Wright Whirlwind 200hp engines – one mounted in the nose, and two slung under the wings. In the cabin there was accommodation for eight passengers, with two pilots in an enclosed cockpit at the front.

Later modifications to the wings, and uprated engines saw the Tri-Motor capable of carrying up to fifteen passengers. Future variants would each adapt the design slightly to try and raise the capabilities of the aircraft, which had already found use not only in carrying passengers and mail, but in supporting crop spraying, mining operations, firefighting, paratrooping and military transport. This was made possible as the

Despite its tank-like appearance, the Ford Tri-Motor was remarkably light and nimble. Like his cars, Henry Ford designed it to be reliable, inexpensive and easy to build.

aircraft's seats were designed to be easily removed when space in the cabin was needed. The aircraft could even be fitted with skis or floats for operation out of frozen ground or water.

The use of corrugated aluminium in the wings and fuselage of the Ford Tri-Motor gave it increased strength and durability, although it was not a new concept and Henry Ford was successfully sued by Junkers in Germany for copying its idea. Nevertheless, always the salesman, Henry Ford made the claim of his aircraft that it was 'the safest airliner around', and it certainly was popular with passengers and the 100 airlines around the world that flew it.

When production ceased in 1933, 199 Ford Tri-Motors had been built. Despite the durability that would see them soldier on for decades to come, new advances in technology meant more modern types would take centre stage.

The Ford Tri-Motor was one of the most iconic American airliners of the era. (Author's collection)

You might be forgiven for wondering why an aircraft that saw only three examples built and enjoyed very limited operational service should be included in a history of the world's most influential airliners. In the case of the Dornier Do X, it is the sheer audacity and ambition of its design that qualifies it for inclusion, as its luxury and scale were beyond compare.

Built at the company's Altenrhein factory on Lake Constance, the Do X actually contravened the Treaty of Versailles because it exceeded speed and range limits imposed on Germany after the First World War.

This aircraft, which could only be described as a leviathan, was a flying boat with six Bristol Jupiter radial engines mounted on top of the high wing.

Below, the cabin could accommodate sixty-six passengers, plus crew, in lavish saloons and seating areas. It copied the luxury of the ocean liners of the time, with dining rooms, cabins, and areas of storage and offices for crew.

Ever been on a flight that seemed to drag on forever? Consider the Dornier Do X, which took nine months to complete its crossing of the Atlantic.

The Dornier Do X, which could only be described as a leviathan, was a flying boat with six Bristol Jupiter radial engines mounted on top of the high wing. (Author's collection)

The Do X made its first flight in July 1929, and later that year actually broke all records for the number of passengers carried on an aircraft when 169 were accommodated on board.

It was intended that the Do X would usher in a new era of luxurious air travel across the Atlantic; however, the flight to prove the route actually took nine months to complete, with the aircraft laid up in New York a further nine months whilst modifications and repairs were carried out. During this time thousands of people flocked to tour the aircraft at Glenn Curtiss Airport.

Delays such as these, and damage caused during a landing incident in 1932, reduced interest in the giant flying boat. Only two further examples were built.

Prior to the Second World War, Germany's aircraft manufacturing industry was growing, producing a number of ever more capable transport aircraft that could fulfil many different roles, from passenger and mail transport to general cargo and military uses.

Junkers in Dessau had already produced a series of important aircraft and, in 1930, set about expanding upon the W 33 aircraft by designing an all-metal transport plane. Like the Ford Tri-Motor that had recently emerged from the United States, the new Ju 52 would include a corrugated metal fuselage and, after abandoning the idea of using a single engine, would make use of two wing-mounted engines and one mounted in the aircraft's nose.

The result was a sturdy, durable aeroplane capable of carrying a useful payload of cargo or up to eighteen passengers from rough airstrips or commercial airports. Its range was more than 600 miles (1,000km) and it was regarded as easy to fly.

With the onset of the Second World War, the Junkers Ju 52 was press-ganged into military service as the transport mode of choice for the Luftwaffe (it had even acted as Hitler's personal transport during his election campaign). More than 2,800 were built during the war years and it saw service in many campaigns, even being used on bombing raids. It was a simple, yet highly effective aircraft.

After the war the Ju 52 saw service in numerous air forces around Europe, including Portugal, Spain and Switzerland. The aircraft was built under licence in countries such as France and Spain.

It was the versatility of the Ju 52 that made it so noteworthy and, mostly due to the war effort, it was Germany's most successful airliner. Its durability meant some were still performing duties into the 1980s, and a number still operate pleasure flights to this day.

Passengers enter the corrugated fuselage of the Junkers Ju 52. (Author's collection)

German operator Lufthansa flew many all-metal Ju 52s. (Author's collection)

Prior to the early mass-produced piston airliners such as the Douglas DC-3, passenger transport types were fairly crude in design, made of wood and not built in huge numbers. However, Boeing changed that when it created its Model 247 airliner.

This low-wing metal aircraft is largely credited as being the first modern passenger airliner, and it paved the way for all future designs, marking a turning point in speed, reliability and on-board comfort.

The Model 247 entered service in 1933 with United Airlines and instantly brought the cross-country journey time between New York and Los Angeles down to twenty hours and fewer stops; a journey that had previously taken well over a day, with a laborious route and the need to find overnight accommodation.

United Airlines was an operator of the Boeing 247.
(San Diego Air & Space Museum Archives)

Of particular importance with this aircraft was its speed. It featured two piston engines with variable pitch propellers, allowing the aircraft to travel at up to 190mph (307km/h). This was also helped by wheels that would partially retract into the engines, thus reducing drag, and de-icing 'boots' on the wings to help prevent the build-up of ice.

The all-metal design offered increased structural strength and reliability in the airframe. It also allowed the cabin to feature air conditioning and sound proofing to reduce the ambient noise level. There was even the novelty of a lavatory on board.

The Boeing 247 was not built in huge numbers, with some seventy-five examples rolling off the production line for various operators, mostly in the United States and China. However, the legacy of the aircraft and its new design was in how it influenced all future passenger airliners going forward.

The incorporation of safe, strong fuselage and wing structures, auto-pilot, retractable landing gear, wing-mounted engines and a comfortable cabin were all unique to the Boeing 247, but became standard for future designs. Without it we would not have had such important and successful airliners as the Douglas DC-2 and DC-3, which went on to revolutionise air travel and bring it to the masses, and which used the same basic layout and features of the 247.

The Boeing 247 is credited as being the first modern airliner. (San Diego Air & Space Museum Archives)

DOUGLAS DC-2

Donald Douglas set up his aircraft company in 1920 and in 1933, despite initial scepticism, responded to a request by TWA for a new airliner capable of carrying twelve passengers from any airport on its network. Using his significant flying experience, he proposed an all-metal aeroplane with a comfortable, heated cabin, variable pitch propellers, stressed aluminium skin and good performance from its engines. This aircraft was the DC-1, which set the ball rolling for one of the most successful series of airliners of all time.

Because United Airlines had exclusive use at the time for Boeing's Model 247 airliner, which had proven a popular and reliable aircraft, TWA wanted to compete with its own aircraft. Only a single DC-1 was built, but TWA was happy with it and, after a few modifications, the production model was being delivered – now named the DC-2. It could carry fourteen passengers, featured retractable landing gear and had more powerful engines.

Not limited to one airline, the Douglas DC-2 saw orders coming from airlines in Europe as well as America, plus a significant order from the United States Air Force. All in all, 130 DC-2s were built.

The DC-2 would quickly be overshadowed by its larger successor, the DC-3, but its importance to flying should not be forgotten. KLM, the national airline of the Netherlands, began a strong association with the Douglas plane, flying it in the London to Melbourne Air Race of 1934 and finishing in second place. The airline would use its DC-2s on the long journey linking Amsterdam to Indonesia (then the Dutch East Indies) and Sydney, flying passengers in comfort and speed.

KLM entered the London to Melbourne Air Race with a Douglas DC-2 in 1934, finishing in second place. (Author)

The Douglas DC-2 and later DC-3 were pioneers of air travel. (Author)

Complete books can be, and are, written on the history and significance of the Douglas DC-3 and its impact on air travel. It was one of the first modern airliners, and led a double life by helping to win a war. While there are many important types in the history of flying that undoubtedly deserve their merit for introducing new technology, flying further, or proving a perfect match for passengers and airlines, the DC-3 is arguably the one that will be top of the pile.

On the back of the DC-2 airliner, Donald Douglas was persuaded that improvements could be made. Interestingly, he had doubts about whether enough DC-3s could be sold to justify the development costs, however this was not the case and airlines loved the type. It was C.R. Smith, the CEO of American Airlines, who talked Douglas into developing a larger version of the DC-2 that could better accommodate sleeper bunks and thus allow greater comfort on cross-country flights. It was initially called the Douglas Sleeper Transport, or DST, and entered service in December 1935. A version with seats instead of bunks followed immediately, which was named the DC-3.

Little fanfare surrounded the first flight and deliveries of the DST, nor its adaptation into the DC-3. However, it seemed that the timing of its introduction was perfect, for more than 400 examples were ordered in its early days by all the main US airlines. It proved adaptable at flying both short- and long-haul routes across the country, opening up new destinations and replacing ageing aircraft that were uncomfortable and loss-making. For the first time airlines could make money flying only passengers, for the DC-3 only cost around 71.6 US cents per mile to operate, yet it accommodated more passengers than previous aircraft. It allowed cross-country flights in as little as seventeen hours with three stops, versus the thirty-eight hours (combined with a train journey) of predecessors such as the Ford Tri-Motor.

As well as comfortable passenger cabins, the DC-3 was used as a troop transport during the Second World War. (Author)

The rich and famous loved it, and the DC-3 was considered so safe that flight insurance was offered for the first time in 1937, and this was also now available to pilots. In fact, by 1939 the DC-3 was responsible for 90 per cent of the world's air passenger traffic, mostly because of its ability to turn a profit for airlines that no longer needed to rely on carrying mail and cargo to supplement their income.

With war looming, the adaptability of the DC-3 came into its own. While civilian examples were only produced until 1943, the production of military variants took over to support the war in Europe and Asia. More than 10,000 aircraft were built for this purpose, taking as little as thirty-four minutes to assemble one aircraft during peak production. Given the military designation C-47 and named the Skytrain and Dakota by different air forces, its ability to transport troops and cargos of different sizes, and also to act as a paratrooper platform, made it invaluable to the war effort. Additionally, more than 5,000 DC-3s were built under licence in Japan and the Soviet Union during the Second World War.

Popular names for the DC-3 included the Dakota, Gooney Bird and Skytrain. It was one of the most numerous airliners ever built, and played a vital role in the Second World War. Many are still flying today.

With the DC-3 airlines could, for the first time, make money from flying only passengers. (Author's collection)

British Midland began operations with DC-3s before going on to jet airliners. (Author's collection)

Following the war, DC-3s were no longer being built, despite efforts to update the design. The problem for Douglas was that thousands of the aircraft had survived the war and were now being sold off to civilian operators, flooding the market. In countries around the world DC-3s would stimulate the emergence of hundreds of new airlines that could make money from the airliner.

Today many DC-3s are still in use, with one airline flying scheduled services in Canada until recently. An adage that the only replacement for a DC-3 was another DC-3 certainly rang true as many manufacturers tried to design something as durable and popular in the post-war years. It was only the emergence of the turboprop and the jet engine that gave new types an advantage over the legendary aircraft.

Such is the legacy of the DC-3 that many are retained in use in the nostalgic colours of airlines and air forces that flew them in the 1940s. It is relatively easy to take a pleasure flight on one of these DC-3s today, and it is certainly feasible that many will still be flying on the type's 100th anniversary.

Commonly referred to as the 'C' Class flying boat, the Short Empire marked a major advance in the standards of air travel on offer. Developed for Imperial Airways to serve its Empire routes to Africa, Asia and Australia, it was a flying boat that offered space and comfort.

Short Brothers in Belfast faced numerous technical hurdles in meeting the specification for the aircraft put forward by Imperial Airways, for no aircraft of this size had ever been developed before. A flying boat design was chosen because it was felt the specification would not be possible in a land-based aircraft due to its size and weight. However, the four Bristol Pegasus engines would need greater clearance from

An experiment in long-distance flying saw a Short S.20 piggyback an S.23 airliner. (Author's collection)

Short S.23s offered a saloon, aft cabin, toilets and galley, promenade deck and space for freight, mail and crew. (Author's collection)

the water and thus were placed high above the waterline. This allowed the aircraft to include an upper deck, and it also meant Short Brothers had to develop new techniques during construction, and a new flap arrangement to give the huge aircraft lift at slower speeds without incurring a disruption to the airflow.

The first Short Empire flew in July 1936. Inside it was fitted out with a saloon, aft cabin, toilets and galley, promenade deck and space for freight, mail and crew. Bunks were commonly fitted for sleeper services.

The Short Empire was built alongside the well-known Short Sunderland and Sandringham flying boats, which were pressed into military service during the war. A special 'piggy back' experiment was also trialled, fitting a Short S.20 float plane to the top of a modified S.23 named *Maia*, which allowed longer-distance travel by staging the journey over two aircraft. Although successful trials took place, the onset of war put a halt to its development.

Only forty-two Short Empire class aircraft were built. In addition to Imperial Airways (which later became BOAC) they flew with Qantas Empire Airways, the Royal Air Force and Royal Australian Air Force. The Second World War saw production cease, and post-war developments in airliners meant a shift away from the size and opulence of the flying boats in favour of economical land-based airliners that could fly further.

two

POST-WAR AIRLINERS

More accurately known as the Beechcraft Model 18, this is a twin-piston engine utility aircraft that emerged in its original form in 1937 at the manufacturer's production plant in Wichita, Kansas.

The 18 is a tail-dragger – more specifically, an aircraft with its main wheels at the front and a rear wheel under the tail that is used to steer the aircraft on the ground. The tailplane is split into two vertical fins, and the large radial engines sit either side of the cockpit. Many post-ward Beech 18 conversions had nosewheels rather than tailwheels.

More than 9,000 Beech 18s were built between 1937 and 1970, when production finally ceased. In that time, more than 4,500 examples were built for military service, with the aircraft used in many roles, such as transport, bombing and reconnaissance, especially during the Second World War. The Beech 18 was originally built to serve as a feeder airliner, however its capabilities were soon realised and more than thirty different variants were built for different roles, from carrying passengers and freight, to hauling equipment into wilderness airstrips, operating off water and snow, and in flying training.

Many aspiring commercial pilots gained navigation experience or earned their multiple-engine ratings on Beech 18s as they found their way into flying schools. Today, plenty of examples are preserved in museum collections, and a precious few still fly as part of vintage collections or even in commercial service in some remote locations.

A Beech 18 wearing military markings. (Author)

The Beech 18 proved a versatile twin-engine aircraft suitable for all manner of operators. (Author)

A preserved Beech 18.
(Author)

More than 9,000 Beech 18s were built between 1937 and 1970.
(Author's collection)

BOEING 307 STRATOLINER

In 1935 Boeing introduced the B-17 Flying Fortress heavy bomber aircraft, which would go on to play an important role in the Second World War. Utilising the design, the Seattle-based manufacturer felt a natural progression into a civilian airliner could be achieved. The result featured many important milestones that would change passenger aircraft travel forever.

The result of the development was the Model 307, to become known as the Stratoliner, which first flew in 1938. It included the tail and wings of a B-17 bomber, but with a new fuselage that could accommodate thirty-three passengers and six crew.

For the first time in any commercial transport aircraft, the Stratoliner featured a pressurised cabin. Such a breakthrough meant the aircraft could travel at greater altitude, above the weather that blighted travel in other aircraft, and allowing greater fuel efficiency and speed. Passengers would not feel the effects of a lack of oxygen at such altitude because of the pressurisation, which kept the cabin altitude below 10,000ft.

Another first for the Stratoliner was the inclusion of a flight engineer as a third cockpit crew member. This had only been seen on flying boats previously, but would become common in land-based airliners for many years to come.

The onset of the Second World War hampered the Stratoliner, but it did enter service with Pan American and TWA before the United States Air Force press-ganged the aircraft into military service for transporting troops across the Atlantic.

The Stratoliner used the wings and tail of a B-17 bomber. (Charles M. Daniels/San Diego Air & Space Museum Archives)

LOCKHEED CONSTELLATION/SUPER CONSTELLATION

Famous aviator and airline entrepreneur Howard Hughes was behind the proposal for one of the most recognisable and successful of the early piston airliners. His airline, Transcontinental and Western Air (better known as TWA) needed a fast, comfortable airliner capable of carrying forty passengers on longer distance routes, including non-stop trips across the Atlantic. American manufacturer Lockheed responded to the proposal with its Constellation design; however, it had even greater ambitions for the new aircraft, with chief engineer Kelly Johnson stating it 'would carry more people farther and faster than ever before, and economically enough to broaden the acceptance of flying as an alternative to train, ship and automobile'.

This aircraft had a top speed of 350mph, which was as fast as a wartime fighter aircraft, and the ability to fly high above the weather thanks to a pressurised cabin.

TWA's bitter rival, Pan American, was also impressed with the proposal and placed its own order. However, before the Constellation could enter service, the United States entered the Second World War and the first aircraft off the production line was pressed straight into a military transport role in January 1943.

Two years later, Lockheed was free to resume selling its Constellation to civil customers once more. Existing military production models were converted to carry passengers, and both Pan American and TWA received their first aircraft.

The Constellation has a distinctive shape, with a bulbous forward fuselage that tapers to a point at the tail, and three vertical fins spread across a wide horizontal stabiliser.

On the wings are four Wright radial engines, and the whole airframe sits atop tall landing gear struts, giving plenty of ground clearance.

A 1962 scene of TWA aircraft at San Francisco Airport, including two L-1049G Super Constellations. (Jon Proctor)

The Constellation has a distinctive shape, with a bulbous forward fuselage that tapers to a point at the tail, and three vertical fins spread across a wide horizontal stabiliser. (Author's collection)

The timing of the Constellation's entry to service was perfect, attracting airlines around the world that were rebuilding their fleets and route networks. Its ability to travel long distances without technical stops, combined with a spacious and comfortable cabin, made it popular with passengers.

Subsequent variants added greater capacity and engine powerplants, however in 1949 Lockheed set about rectifying early teething problems and higher than anticipated costs by stretching a standard Constellation model by 18ft (5.5m) and adding new 2700hp Wright Cyclone radial engines to add a burst of power. The result was the L-1049 Super Constellation, which could now carry up to ninety-five passengers over distances of up to 4,600 miles (7,400km) thanks to extra fuel tanks in the wing tips.

The Lockheed Constellation owed its existence to legendary aviator Howard Hughes, who encouraged its development for his airline, TWA. It was easily recognisable by its three vertical tails and fuselage that thinned out towards the end. Three Constellations were used as the presidential airliner for President Dwight D. Eisenhower in the 1950s.

The Super Constellation became the superior variant, proving popular with many of the world's major airlines thanks to its range and lower seat-mile costs. It also featured novel additions such as air conditioning and reclining seats. This stretched variant, distinguished from the original Constellation by a longer rear fuselage and square windows, would see numerous modifications to cater for airline preferences throughout the 1950s.

Lockheed created one final Constellation variant in 1957, named the L-1649 Starliner; however, competition from the new jet airliners drew the attention of airlines away from older generation aircraft. The Super Constellation and its other variants were among the last of the great piston airliners, yet they had proven themselves as some of the most efficient and economic airliners to fly.

BOAC Constellation *Balmoral* landing at London's Heathrow airport.
(Author's collection)

BOEING 377 STRATOCRUISER

Like the Model 307 Stratoliner, Boeing developed the bulbous 377 Stratocruiser out of a military model built for war. The B-29 Superfortress was another heavy bomber used in the Second World War and later conflicts, which stemmed into the C-97 Stratofreighter of 1947. This aircraft was funded largely by the military. In a shrewd move, Boeing employed staff to work on a civil derivative in tandem with the C-97, naming it the Model 377 Stratocruiser.

A Pan American Boeing 377 Stratocruiser about to touch down. (Author's collection)

The Stratocruiser would not be fully developed until the victory in Japan of August 1945, and it would be a little under two years later the first aircraft flew. Boeing had used all the technological advances made during the war in designing its new passenger aircraft, choosing comfort and elegance to attract airlines and their passengers.

For the first time in a land-plane, the Stratocruiser included two decks for passengers. The lower deck could include sleeper berths or cabins, dressing rooms and a lounge, whilst up to 100 passengers could be seated on the upper deck.

Pan American World Airways committed to the Stratocruiser before it had even flown, placing the largest aircraft order in history at the time for twenty aircraft, valued at more than $24 million.

Despite the large, rounded nose of the Stratocruiser, it could easily cruise at around 300mph (480kmh) over distances of up to 2,750 miles (4,400km). Passengers flying airlines such as American Overseas Airways, BOAC, Northwest Airlines and United Airlines would enjoy years of long-distance travel on these aircraft until the advance of the jet age in the 1950s saw their replacement.

One interesting development of the Stratocruiser was the Aero Spacelines Guppy. Adding a new oversized fuselage and turboprop engines to the existing wings, cockpit and tailplane of the 377, the Guppy models were used to carry aircraft parts, space rockets and other oversized cargo in unique circumstances.

With the seats turned down into beds, the Stratocruiser accommodates its passengers for flying through the night. (San Diego Air & Space Museum Archives)

50 AIRLINERS THAT CHANGED FLYING

A Stratocruiser flying above the clouds.
(Author's collection)

DE HAVILLAND CANADA DHC-2 BEAVER

After the Second World War, de Havilland Canada recognised the need for a bush plane that could replace the aircraft developed previously for the purpose, which had now become quite outdated. The company's response was the DHC-2 Beaver, which first flew in August 1947.

The aircraft's key characteristics were the ability to take off and land in a short distance – so called STOL performance. It would be able to fly from rough, unprepared airstrips and – most importantly – from water when equipped with floats.

The result was an all-metal airframe that could accommodate passengers or bulky cargoes. It had excellent performance, with a single Pratt & Whitney Wasp Junior engine mounted at the front. Its versatility made it the perfect choice for a wide range of operators in Canada's wilderness regions, and the Beaver also became popular in areas such as Alaska and New Zealand.

Production of the DHC-2 ceased in 1967 when the DHC-3 took over. However, of the 1,657 Beavers built, many are still working hard in the environments they were built for. The type has since been voted one of the top ten icons of Canada, and is largely recognised as the most important utility aircraft ever built.

Like the DHC-6 Twin Otter, it is thought that Beaver production may start up again under new licence owners Viking Air.

Of the 1,657 Beavers built, many are still working hard in the rugged environment for which they were built. (Phasmatisnox/Creative Commons)

A float-equipped DHC-2 Beaver operating in Seattle. (Dllu/Creative Commons)

The sight and sound of a DHC-2 Beaver is said to be one of the top ten icons of Canada, such is its importance to the history and culture of the country.

The Beaver was a short take-off and landing, or STOL aircraft, which meant it could use the shortest amount of space to get airborne or land.

One of the most successful utility aircraft the world has ever known, and certainly one of the most successful aircraft developed by the Soviet Union, is the Antonov An-2.

This biplane first flew in 1947, yet incredibly production continued until 2001, with more than 18,000 examples thought to have been built. It arrived at a time when the Soviet Union was recovering from the effects of the Second World War and rebuilding. This was the perfect aircraft to facilitate that.

The key to the success of this aircraft was in its adaptability to any role, and its robustness to operate in any environment. It could just as easily fly commuters between airports as it could operate as a crop sprayer over farmland or haul mining equipment to a remote outpost covered in snow.

The layout of the aircraft and its engine meant the An-2 offered good performance on take-off, even from unprepared runways. It was also affordable to buy, cheap to operate, and did not need to be treated softly.

Antonov An-2s were exported all over the world, finding many different roles. You will still find them flying today – perhaps dropping parachutists or displaying at an air show. It has even been demonstrated as being able to fly backwards when flying into a strong headwind!

The An-2 is said to be the only transport aircraft that can be flown backwards – a feat that has been demonstrated on numerous occasions!

The NATO codename for the An-2 was the Colt. Now, more than seventy years after its first flight, the An-2 is being brought back to life as the TVS-2DTS. It includes brand-new turboprop engines, composite fuselage, new interior and redesigned wings.

Inside the Antonov An-2, which has been used for anything from transporting military equipment to a platform for parachute drops. (Author)

Developed in response to a proposal by Britain's ubiquitous Brabazon Committee, set up during the Second World War to decide future civil aircraft needs, the Vickers Viscount was the world's first airliner designed from the outset to use turboprop engines, replacing the standard piston engine used on all aircraft prior to this.

The Viscount was also designed to be pressurised – a new development pioneered in America, allowing aircraft to fly at greater altitude whilst still allowing passengers to breathe comfortably. Doing so meant a smoother ride above the weather.

The first two aircraft, powered by four Rolls-Royce Dart engines, flew in July 1948. Because of the lukewarm response to it by the national carrier British European Airways (BEA), the designers were given greater freedom in specifying that the production aircraft should be larger, accommodating more passengers. This move undoubtedly made the Viscount a more attractive commercial prospect for other airlines, and it went on to become one of the most successful aircraft not only of the post-war period, but of all time for Britain's airliner manufacturing industry.

The Viscount is the most successful British airliner ever to have been developed. Around 440 were built between 1948 and 1964, with many orders from airlines around the world. The last examples retired in the 2000s.

British European Airways introduced the Vickers Viscount in 1953. (Author)

A later Viscount 800 receiving its passengers. (Author's collection)

The Viscount was one of Britain's most successful airliners. (Author's collection)

Work on the de Havilland Comet aircraft actually began before the end of the Second World War, when the Brabazon Committee asked for manufacturers to propose a new commercial airliner for BOAC, the national airline, that could cross the Atlantic in comfort at 500mph.

de Havilland, based at Hatfield to the north of London, had the winning proposal and would change the face of flying with its design, for it would become the world's first jet-powered airliner. Prior to this point, every aircraft to carry passengers had been powered by piston engines, yet a new era was dawning: jet technology was impacting fighter aircraft design, and the British aircraft manufacturing industry was seen as the best in the world for technological innovation.

Key to the success of the Comet design, which had the designation DH.106 (every de Havilland aircraft had a successive model number), was the four Ghost turbo jet engines buried into the wing root close to the fuselage. Described as 'ear splitting' for those on the ground, they allowed the aircraft to travel at speed, carrying thirty-six passengers in comfort.

Having first flown on 27 July 1949, the important moment arrived on 2 May 1952 when fare-paying passengers flew on a jetliner for the first time. The route was from London's Heathrow Airport to Johannesburg, with various stops along the way. The world was watching, and the aircraft was soon profitable for BOAC, with some 30,000 passengers carried in the first year (including Queen Elizabeth and members of the royal family). Comets could be seen across the Empire routes of Asia and Africa.

Yet, even with such pioneering technology, the Comet was prone to some unfortunate accidents. Early incidents saw aircraft lost in take-off crashes due to a design flaw in the wing, whilst another was lost when it disintegrated in a thunderstorm near Calcutta.

A longer Comet 4 example, which could carry more passengers and fly further than previous Comets. (Author's collection)

The prototype Comet 1, which was the world's first pressurised jet airliner. (Author's collection)

Then, in 1954, two Comets were lost within three months, both shortly after departing from Rome. In both cases the aircraft crashed into the Mediterranean Sea, killing all on board, and speculation over the cause was rife. Following the second crash the Comet's certificate of airworthiness was revoked pending an enquiry, and all production ceased on new aircraft.

With sections of the second aircraft recovered for investigation, as well as pressurisation tests on a similar aircraft in a water tank, the committee established to find the cause of the crashes soon discovered significant weaknesses in the skin of the aircraft. Of particular concern was the area around the windows along the fuselage, where squared corners were a point at which cracks would appear under the repeated stress of pressurisation and depressurisation during a flight. In the case of the

Following a number of incidents with early Comets, the Comet 4 was introduced with greater capacity, and rounded windows that would not suffer pressure cracks. (Author's collection)

50 AIRLINERS THAT CHANGED FLYING

The Comet was the first jet airliner to enter commercial service. Although not a great sales success, it was a milestone moment for air travel. Despite this, the initial Comet model only had a range of 1,500 miles and had to make several stops on its key routes to Africa and Asia.

crashes near Rome, both aircraft had reached a critical point where the small cracks failed and the aircraft disintegrated in mid-air.

Recommendations were immediately made for future designs. The Comet 1 would never enter service again, but at the time further developments of the Comet were being proposed as new models – the Comet 2 and Comet 3 – offering greater range and increased passenger capacity. Windows would now be rounded instead of square (a feature of all airliners since then), and rivets used to fasten the windows would be drilled instead of punched. Whilst the basic design of the Comet was found to be sound, extra safety measures were introduced, including thicker fuselage skin. Airlines around the world had confirmed orders or shown significant interest for the new Comet 2 and 3, including Air India, Japan Air Lines, National Airlines, Pan American and Qantas. However, following the crashes these orders were cancelled or switched to the newer Comet 4, which was longer and could fly even farther. It first flew in April 1958 and entered service with BOAC on transatlantic flights to New York later that year.

As with many British airliners, the Comet did not see much commercial success. The crashes caused serious harm to its reputation, and by the time the Comet 4 had emerged, rivals across the Atlantic were already enjoying success with their own jet airliners. The Boeing 707 and Douglas DC-8 would be sold in larger numbers, and offered greater capacity and comfort on board.

Nevertheless, the Comet would fly into the 1980s, most notably with British leisure airline Dan-Air London, which snapped up as many second-hand examples as it could find to operate holiday charters.

The Comet would also be the basis for the design of the Nimrod maritime patrol aircraft used by the Royal Air Force from 1969. The final incarnation of this heavily modified aircraft would be cancelled in 2010, some sixty-one years after the Comet first flew.

Despite its limited commercial success, the Comet's place in history is firmly set. It allowed travel around the world at a greater pace than ever before, harnessing the comfort and service levels of the previous generations of airliner and the technological advances of the jet engine. It drew crowds wherever it went, and flew higher and faster than any aircraft before. Until the fatigue failures it was regarded as a perfect aeroplane, and it will always be the first pressurised jet airliner.

The de Havilland Comet beat all others to usher in the age of jet airline travel, but the Boeing 707 would be the aircraft that truly brought the jet age to life. With its sleek lines, swept wings and engines slung underneath, it seemed to capture the imagination of the public in a way not seen since the era of the flying boats.

Knowing the future of commercial travel was in jet-powered aircraft, and having seen the work of the British and other manufacturers in making it a reality, the board of Boeing in Seattle decided in 1952 to go ahead with a proposal for a large airliner nicknamed the 'Dash 80', but given the official designation Boeing model 367-80.

In the 1950s Boeing was a big name in the world of military aircraft, but was not yet on the world stage with its passenger airliners. At the time Douglas was the major player, having set the world alight with its DC-3 and later piston airliners, whilst Lockheed would make waves with its Constellation airliner. However, Boeing had the well-known designer Ed Wells on board for its new jet airliner. Walls was behind the B-17 Flying Fortress, B-29 Superfortress and B-52 Stratofortress – all successful, large aircraft.

The costs involved in developing such a project would put the company at risk (a feat that would be repeated in the 1960s with the 747 jumbo jet). Boeing wanted to build the most advanced airliner possible, with plenty of cabin space and speed, and make it a reliable workhorse that could operate anywhere in the world.

When the aircraft first flew in 1954, it had cost the company $16 million to develop over two years and still had no committed customers. It was designed to be developed into both a commercial airliner and an airborne refuelling tanker for military service.

The resulting commercial airliner that would come from the Dash 80 prototype was named the Boeing 707 and entered service in October 1958

with Pan American, which had saved the project by ordering twenty aircraft (as well as twenty-five of the rival Douglas DC-8).

The layout chosen for the aircraft was for wings swept back at a 35 degree angle, with four engines slung in pods underneath. These turbofan engines, initially supplied by Pratt & Whitney, supplied pressurised air to the passenger cabin, and also featured clam-shell style thrust reversers to help the aircraft slow on landing.

Inside the cabin there was room for 174 passengers in a six-abreast layout (three seats either side of an aisle). Later variants would offer an additional twenty seats.

It was Pan American that contributed significantly to the magic that came to surround the 707 when it entered service. Passengers were thrilled at the on-board service, the glamour of the pilots and cabin crew, and the speed and comfort at which it could whisk passengers between destinations. Although developed for the short- to medium-haul market, the 707 would become popular flying greater distances, such as between North America and Europe, and on the round-the-world networks of Pan Am and TWA.

The craze of the Boeing 707 would also enter popular culture, referred to in song, featuring in movies and even purchased as a private jet by Frank Sinatra (the same aircraft was later owned by John Travolta). Later, when an Iranian airline became the last operator of a passenger 707, enthusiasts would flock to the country just to experience a flight on the aircraft.

While the de Havilland Comet had been a commercial failure, and was dogged by a number of fatal accidents, Boeing undoubtedly created a commercial success out of its 707. Not necessarily a big money spinner, it still garnered more orders than the rival DC-8, which entered service less than a year later.

Boeing 707 aircraft gather at New York's JFK airport in the company of a Vickers VC10, the less successful British rival. (Peter Black/Jon Proctor Collection)

Although branded a Boeing 707, this aircraft is in fact a Boeing 720, the smaller, shorter-range variant popular with America's main airlines. (Jon Proctor)

Boeing 707s of Dan-Air London and Pan American grace the apron at Prestwick Airport. (Author's collection)

To remain competitive and adapt to customer feedback and wishes, Boeing created different variants of its 707, from the original -120, to the popular -320, the Rolls-Royce-powered -420, and the shorter-range -020 (usually named the Boeing 720).

All in all, just over 1,000 Boeing 707s rolled off the production line between 1958 and 1978, alongside 800 military variants.

Interestingly, the legacy of the 707 lives on in many of the subsequent airliners produced by Boeing. It was used in testing parts and systems for the 727 and 737, and its basic fuselage and nose designs are almost identical on these types, and can still be seen today on the thousands of 737s flying.

By today's standards, the 707 is of a different era. It was noisy, trailed smoke, had limited range and first-generation engines. However, there is no question that it changed flying for millions of people. Despite not being the first jet airliner, it somehow managed to catapult airlines into the jet age by selling more than any jet airliner had at the time. Its shape was instantly recognisable and will endure as a symbol of flight for many years to come.

During the early days of jet aircraft, the Soviet Union's experienced aircraft manufacturing industry was keen to keep up with developments in the West. Tupolev produced the strategic, long-range Tu-16 bomber with engines embedded into its wings. To simultaneously keep up with commercial aircraft developments, the manufacturer took the Tu-16 and added a new, wider fuselage on to the tail and wings of the bomber to create the country's first jet airliner, given the Tu-104 model number.

The initial design was not quite up to standard, and so Tupolev stretched the fuselage to allow up to 115 passengers to be carried on the Tu-104B variant. It could also fly up to an altitude of 39,000ft at great speed. However, the primitive wings and braking systems of the day meant the manufacturers needed to install brake parachutes that were deployed upon landing to help slow the aircraft down before it reached the end of the runway.

Although the Tu-104 came after the de Havilland Comet and Sud Aviation Caravelle early jet airliners, for a two-year period between 1956 and 1958 it was the world's only operational jet airliner. This occurred when the Comet was grounded owing to safety concerns following two crashes, and was before the Caravelle entered airline service.

Such was the secrecy of this new Russian jet that when a Tu-104 flew into London Heathrow airport for the first time in 1956, journalists and engineers were keen to get a glimpse of it to understand the Soviet design advances, and how they had approached developing jet airliners.

The Tu-104 was undoubtedly a success. It took the Soviet Union's already comprehensive experience in airliner development into the jet age, and allowed safe, comfortable travel for passengers travelling around the huge country on the national airline Aeroflot. Further modifications would see the regional Tu-124 developed, before Tupolev hit the big time with its Tu-134 and Tu-154 airliners in the 1960s.

The Tupolev Tu-104 took the Soviet Union into the jet age.

SUD AVIATION CARAVELLE

The Caravelle was an airliner developed in France in the early days of jet-powered passenger aircraft. Unlike the pioneering British de Havilland Comet, which was the first passenger jet airliner, and the longer-range Boeing 707 and Douglas DC-8 airliners being developed in the United States, the Caravelle was designed from the outset to target the short- to medium-haul market. This led to early interest from some key airlines, including Air France, Finnair, Swissair, SAS, and even United Airlines in the lucrative American market.

For the first time ever, Sud Aviation introduced the idea of attaching the turbofan engines that would power the Caravelle at the rear of the fuselage, which in turn saw the relocation of the horizontal stabiliser higher up the tail plane. It meant a quieter, faster ride for passengers.

The Caravelle first flew in 1955 and was considered the first successful jet airliner to be developed in mainland Europe. It was still common to see later variants of Caravelle flying into the 1990s, particularly with leisure airlines ferrying holidaymakers from Northern Europe to sunnier destinations. However, one of its key legacies would come from the influence it had on the emergence of Airbus, which was founded by one of the Caravelle's engineers, Roger Béteille.

At first glance, the cockpit and nose of the Caravelle may look familiar. That's because it was a direct copy of the de Havilland Comet, owing to a license agreement between the two manufacturers that saw the nose and cockpit of the British jet used by the French.

Air Inter was a French airline that flew Caravelle aircraft. (Author's collection)

The Caravelle was the first airliner to feature jet engines positioned on the rear of the fuselage. (Author's collection)

The Caravelle first flew in 1955 and
was considered the first successful
jet airliner to be developed on
mainland Europe.
(Author's collection)

Sud Aviation Caravelle cockpit.
(Author)

When the world emerged from war in the late 1940s, there was a surplus of piston-engine airliners available for passenger use. As a result many new airlines started up, taking advantage of the relatively cheap costs of acquiring aircraft. Many aircraft manufacturers predicted that these wartime aircraft would soon need to be replaced by modern, more comfortable airliners and set about designing their offerings. We can thank this period for aircraft such as the Vickers Viscount, Handley Page Herald, Avro 748 and Lockheed Electra. In the Netherlands, Dutch manufacturer Fokker was working on its own new airliner that, like many others, would use the new turboprop technology instead of piston engines. The result was the F27 Friendship, which first flew in November 1955.

As well as these new engines, the aircraft was designed to work on rough strips and airports without service vehicles, with high wings supported by strong, long landing gear. The fuselage was low to the ground, meaning steps were not needed. Inside, a passenger cabin capable of holding up to fifty-six passengers was comfortable, and thanks to the Rolls-Royce Dart engines the airliner could fly up to 286mph. It could therefore just as easily be found flying from major hub airports as it could remote regions of Africa or Asia.

Of all the post-war airliners that set about tempting new airline orders, the F27 was the most successful. It sold more than 580 examples, alongside more than 200 licence-built examples, and was adapted into the Fokker 50 in the 1980s that sold a further 213 examples.

The Fokker 50 prototype on display in the Netherlands. (Author)

Some F27s were built under licence in the USA as Fairchild FH-227s. (Author's collection)

50 AIRLINERS THAT CHANGED FLYING

Perfect for short regional flights, the F27 was common with commuter airlines. (Author)

The F27 was one of a number of post-war airliners to use the Rolls-Royce Dart turboprop engine. Others included the Vickers Viscount, Avro 748 and Handley Page Herald. The Dart had a familiar whistle sound and it could be heard at airports all over the world.

GRUMMAN GULFSTREAM I

In the years following the Second World War, most aircraft being used for corporate travel comprised surplus military aircraft that had been crudely adapted for this work. They were outdated, using older piston technology, and not particularly comfortable.

Grumman Aircraft Engineering Corporation decided that it could develop its C-1 Trader aircraft into a new design that was built specifically for the corporate market. Named the Gulfstream, it utilised new Dart turboprop engines from Rolls-Royce that gave it speed, and a low wing to allow more space in the cabin. It first flew in August 1958.

The Gulfstream became the first corporate aircraft certified to operate up to 30,000ft, and could comfortably fly distances up to 2,500 miles (4,000km). A stretched variant was introduced that opened the Gulfstream to the airline market, capable of flying up to twenty-four passengers for regional services, or an equivalent amount of cargo.

However, the basic fuselage design would go on to inspire a whole range of business jets, both in the Gulfstream range and from rival manufacturers, built solely with corporate travel in mind. From the jet-powered Gulfstream II in 1966 to the recent G600, it was this first aircraft that brought economics, good design and style together for this particular market.

The turboprop-powered Gulfstream would go on to inspire many future corporate jets.
(Author's collection)

Between the 1930s and 1950s, the Douglas Aircraft Company had engineered for itself an enviable position as the most successful manufacturer of transport aircraft, which were still proving popular with operators around the world. The company's stable of popular piston airliners included the DC-3, DC-4, DC-6 and DC-7, which saw both civil and military service. However, the company recognised the importance of staying current, and set about its entry into the jet age on the back of Britain and France doing so with their Comet and Caravelle airliners.

French Air Force Douglas DC-8 on display in Paris. (Author)

Part of the success of the DC-8 was in the later stretched variants. (Author's collection)

The DC-8 was operated all over the world. (Author's collection)

Initially Douglas was competing for a US Air Force contract to build a jet tanker, but this would awarded to Boeing, so Douglas chose to carry on with its designs, which would become the DC-8.

The airliner was designed at a similar time to Boeing's 707. Both would take earlier jet designs to a new level, choosing to produce larger aircraft with four engines slung underneath the wing, and designing their aircraft to have a range capable of crossing the North Atlantic or the continental United States. It would be offered in four different sizes, all with the same cabin width, but incorporating a different length to accommodate more passengers, greater fuel capacity and different engine specifications.

Despite lagging behind the Boeing 707, the Douglas DC-8 managed to secure a number of high-profile airline orders during the development phase. This gave the company a boost, ahead of the first prototype appearing in April 1958, nearly two years behind the prototype 707.

The DC-8 was very much in the first generation of jet airliners. It utilised turbofan engines that were noisy and smoky, and fuel economies were much worse than those of today's airliners. However, this aircraft adapted to provide better performance, greater range and capacity, and other improvements requested by airlines over subsequent variants to make it a very successful airliner that had a reputation for reliability and strength.

The arrival of the DC-10 following the merger of McDonnell and Douglas put the DC-8 out to pasture, yet many of the 556 examples built soldiered on into the 1990s and 2000s.

As with so many British airliner designs, the success was not in sales but in the advances it brought. In the case of the 1950s-designed Vickers VC10, it was also in the sheer elegance of its lines and the era in which it flew. Many today will remember taking a VC10 to hot and dusty destinations in Africa and the Middle East towards the end of the period where passengers still dressed up for a flight.

As a result of being funded by the British government, the VC10 took much of its design from the requirements of BOAC for a jet airliner capable of flying from 'hot and high' airfields with short runways on its Empire routes.

The resulting design was this sleek airliner with a high T-tail and four rear-mounted engines, sat on a tall, strong undercarriage. It could easily carry a full payload from the short runways at airports such as Nairobi, Entebbe or Karachi, which was a major bonus for airlines on these routes. A stretched Super VC10 was also developed, which became popular on the London to New York route during the 1970s.

However, the delay in bringing the VC10 into service allowed the Boeing 707 and Douglas DC-8 to capture a much larger slice of the market – especially with major airlines such as Pan Am, TWA and Qantas. Even BOAC ordered the 707. Despite these rivals being technologically inferior in many ways, when airports starting building longer runways the VC10's superiorities in this respect were no longer as important.

In later years the VC10 was a key component of the Royal Air Force, used as both a troop transporter and air-to-air refuelling tanker. The last examples were retired in 2013.

Vickers VC10 passenger cabin. (Author)

A preserved British Airways VC10. (Author)

The VC10 enjoyed a renaissance as a Royal Air Force tanker and troop-transport aircraft. (Author)

Gulf Air VC10. (Author's collection)

The VC10 was Britain's answer to the big American jets like the Boeing 707. It was a passenger and pilot favourite, and advertising slogans at the time included phrases such as 'Try a little VC10derness'.

three

JUMBOS, MASS TRAVEL AND UTILITY AIRCRAFT

The Hawker Siddeley Trident is an example of how the measure of an aircraft's success is not solely down to the number of aircraft sold.

This pioneering British design should have been a world-beater, addressing many advances in technology and safety that are still present on the airliners we travel on today.

When the specification for the Trident first hit the design boards in 1957, it was in the offices of de Havilland and designated the DH.121. However, by the time it saw the light of day the company had been merged into Hawker Siddeley and all aircraft were given the HS. designator.

At the time, British aircraft manufacturers competed for tenders to develop new aircraft for the national airlines. The Trident was the result of a proposal by British European Airways (BEA) for an airliner that could meet a series of changing requirements for its own network. However, because of BEA's increasingly uncommercial requests, the Trident found itself pushed out of contention with most of the other airlines that would otherwise have been interested in ordering it for their own fleets. This blinkered view would ultimately see only 117 Tridents being built, starting with the initial 1C model and ranging through three later variants. By the time the stretched Trident 3B had been built, offering a much more competitive range and passenger capacity, Boeing's own tri-jet 727 design was setting the world alight and attracting many more orders.

Nevertheless, the Trident's sales failures pale into insignificance when you look at its technological advances, for while the designers were grappling with BEA's demands, they also saw the chance to develop triplicated systems for added safety. Alongside the three tail-mounted engines, the Trident featured a revolutionary automatic landing system that allowed it to land in near zero-visibility conditions with no hands-on input from the pilots. This gave airlines a major advantage over their

The Trident also enjoyed orders from the Chinese national airline. (Author's collection)

Hawker Siddeley's Trident was the first airliner that could perform a completely automated landing. (Author's collection)

A line-up of Tridents at Heathrow in the 1960s. (Author's collection)

The nosewheel of the Trident was offset to one side, giving it an uneven appearance when seen head-on. The reason for this was that the equipment developed to allow the aircraft to land on autopilot was so large that the wheel had to retract sideways instead of forwards, as is normal.

competitors, reducing delays for its passengers when landing in foggy conditions, which were prevalent at airports such as London Heathrow.

Another first for the Trident was in the use of quick-access flight data recorders (so-called black boxes) to capture a record of each flight, which could be analysed in the event of an accident to determine the cause.

Tridents were retired in Europe in 1985, with some Chinese examples flying on into the 1990s. Yet even in retirement, a grounded Trident airliner was used to develop the floor-level lighting now used in aircraft to direct passengers towards emergency exits in the dark or when smoke fills the cabin.

While Britain and the United States were perfecting their long-haul airliner designs, the Soviet Union was not far behind in matching the achievements of the West. Its proposal for a large airliner capable of travelling long distance was the Ilyushin Il-62, seen as the successor to the Il-18 turboprop aircraft from the 1950s.

When it first flew in January 1963, the Il-62 was the world's largest airliner. Its distinct shape, with a large T-tail and four rear-mounted engines, immediately drew comparisons with the Vickers VC10 alongside cries of espionage, especially considering the similar development periods and unique shape. However, there were enough differences between the two aircraft (including many superiorities found in the Il-62) to satisfy many that the Soviet aircraft was merely great minds thinking alike.

The Il-62 was popular with airlines in Eastern Europe and Asia and carried up to 198 passengers. It was the standard Russian long-range aircraft for many years, and could cover distances such as Moscow to New York or the Caribbean (via a diplomatic stop in Ireland). However, few Westerners got the opportunity to fly on the Il-62, unlike the more common Tupolev Tu-154 medium-haul airliners.

Many Soviet-era aircraft bear a striking resemblance to counterparts from the West. However, few are so strikingly similar as the Il-62, which has the same tall T-tail and four rear-mounted engines as the Vickers VC10. Despite this, most Soviet airliners had many original features.

Many Soviet Bloc
nations operated the
Il-62, such as CSA
Czechoslovakia Airlines.
(Jimmy Wadia)

Aeroflot was the
principal operator of the
Ilyushin Il-62.
(Author's collection)

It is said that engineers from Boeing visited the factory of Hawker Siddeley in the United Kingdom at the time it was developing its revolutionary Trident airliner (see Hawker Siddeley HS.121 Trident). They went away and designed their own aircraft, which looked remarkably similar and offered much of the same technology.

Whatever the truth in the story, Boeing achieved something incredible with the 727, which seemed to resonate with the market at the time. The Trident may have introduced many of the technologies we take for granted in airliners today, yet it failed to reach the mark in terms of sales. However, Boeing managed to create a stir with the 727 that ultimately saw more than 1,800 examples being built – a record for many years.

The T-tail aircraft had three rear-mounted engines. One of its major selling points was its ability to take off in a much shorter distance than the previous generation of jet airliners, such as the 707 and Douglas DC-8. This opened up a range of new airports to jet airline service, which was the buzz word with passengers at the time.

The 727 first flew in February 1963, with a stretched model becoming standard from 1967. It found huge success with airlines in the United States for operators on trunk. It would also prove popular with major airlines around the world, giving an economic range of up to 2,500 miles with up to 189 passengers on board.

Production of the 727 ceased in 1984, superseded by the popular 737 and new 757 aircraft. Yet the 727 would remain common into the 2000s, with some cargo examples still flying today.

Boeing 727s still flying today have diverse roles, including as oil spill response aircraft that can spray dispersants. (Author)

Even Donald Trump utilised Boeing 727s for his Trump Shuttle service between cities of the north-east United States. (Author's collection)

All the major US airlines operated the Boeing 727 in great numbers. (Author's collection)

The 727 included a door and staircase underneath the tail, allowing access to the aircraft from the rear. In 1971 a hijacker named D.B. Cooper used this entrance to parachute from a 727 high over Oregon with a suitcase full of money. He was never seen again.

The One-Eleven was designed by the new British Aircraft Corporation (which had been formed as an amalgamation of English Electric, Vickers-Armstrong, Hunting Aircraft and the Bristol Aeroplane Company) in the early 1960s. It was intended as a replacement for Britain's most popular airliner to date, the Vickers Viscount, and it also drew heavily on the recent jet designs of the Sud Aviation Caravelle in France, and Hawker Siddeley's Trident. Evidence of this is in the fad of the day, rear-mounted engines and a T-tail configuration.

The One-Eleven was actually developed as a smaller alternative to the Vickers VC10 longer range airliner, to give airlines a choice for shorter regional routes, settling on a capacity of close to ninety passengers. It first flew in August 1963, two years before the Douglas DC-9, which resembles the British aircraft closely.

One of the keys to the success of the One-Eleven was in it not being designed to a specification from the state-run airlines BEA and BOAC. Poor sales of the Trident and VC10 had been attributed to this, and subsequently the One-Eleven went on to see success with orders from the United States – the first time with a British jet airliner. When production ceased in the United Kingdom in 1982, some models continued to be built under licence in Romania until 1989.

When mainline carriers such as British Airways and Aer Lingus retired their aircraft, the One-Eleven soldiered on in the service of smaller independent airlines, particularly common on holiday charters, until the final examples were retired in the early 2000s due to noise compliance issues.

British Airways operated a large fleet of BAC One-Elevens until the mid-1990s.
(Author's collection)

The One-Eleven offered a rear staircase, allowing passenger access beneath the tail.
(Author's collection)

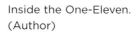

Inside the One-Eleven.
(Author)

50 AIRLINERS THAT CHANGED FLYING

The One-Eleven was popular in many countries as a short- to medium-haul airliner. (Author's collection)

Airlines such as USAir operated the One-Eleven on trunk routes and to regional airports. (Author's collection)

Following the success of the DHC-3 Otter, de Havilland Canada set about designing a follow-up aircraft, this time using turboprop engines for more power and safety. The scope for the DHC-6 Twin Otter was wide ranging, with possibilities to be used for cargo and utility purposes, as a passenger airliner, in military roles, a parachute launch platform, or even in rugged terrain. Operators could easily fly the aircraft from rough ground, fit skis for ice runways, or floats for seaplane operations. Key to its success was in being able to take off in a very short distance.

Built over three models, the first Twin Otter flew in 1965. The DHC-6-300 was the most popular model, offering more powerful engines and increased baggage capacity.

It truly was a workhorse, and became the most successful aircraft built in Canada. More than 800 examples were built for operators in more than eighty countries. Today, long after production ceased in 1988, Twin Otters are still flying in as many diverse roles around the world as the designers had hoped for, including ferrying tourists to island resorts in the Maldives, landing on tiny airstrips in the Caribbean, and even flying the only scheduled beach landing in Scotland.

So popular is the aircraft that the designs were purchased by Viking Air, which has resurrected the Twin Otter in a new variant, with more powerful engines and modern on-board systems. It is now in production once again.

Long after the first production run ceased in 1988, Twin Otters are still flying in many diverse roles around the world. (Author)

Built in three different models, the first Twin Otter flew in 1965. (Author's collection)

Few aircraft could claim to have had such a successful impact on the world of air travel as the Boeing 737. To date it has been the most numerous jet airliner ever built, and is still in production more than fifty years after the first example rolled off the production line.

When the 737 appeared, Boeing had already achieved recent success in the form of the 727, which offered good economics and the ability to fly from shorter runways. However, with the Douglas DC-9 and BAC One-Eleven offering smaller jets, Boeing wanted to make sure it had both segments of the market covered. This was timely as some of its valuable customers had elected for the 727, but would also benefit from something smaller. One of these airlines was Lufthansa, the national carrier of Germany, which became the first to commit to the new 737. It entered service in February 1968. In order to speed up the development and gain valuable time against its competitors, the 737 features many of the same structures and on-board systems as the 727.

The 737 is a single-aisle twin jet, with engines slung under the wing. The initial -100 model could carry up to 118 passengers over a range of 1,540 miles (2,855km). However, United Airlines favoured a slightly larger aircraft capable of carrying up to 130 passengers. Boeing immediately stretched the design to create the 737-200, which became the standard model after the initial batch of -100s had been built.

Surprisingly, sales of the 737 slowed to a trickle in the early 1970s and Boeing considered ending production. However, a flurry of orders came when modifications were offered to enable the type to carry cargo, or a mixture of passengers and cargo, as well as military and 'off-road' gravel runway variants. Sales from European leisure operators also boosted confidence in the type, with carriers such as Britannia Airways using 737s whilst its competitors still flew early generation jets or even piston airliners.

An Aloha Airlines Boeing 737-200 operating inter-island services in Hawaii.
(Author's collection)

Britannia Airways became the first UK airline to fly the Boeing 737, using it on holiday services around Europe.
(Author's collection)

Although more than 1,100 737-200s were built, everything changed for Boeing when it developed the 737-300 and, to a lesser extent, the -400 and -500. These larger aircraft featured new, high-bypass turbofan engines, better aerodynamics and increased passenger capacity. The costs of operating the aircraft were improved, along with its performance and range. Airlines flocked to these new offerings, with orders coming in from around the world following the introduction of the -300 in 1984.

In the late 1980s, Boeing saw a new threat from the other side of the Atlantic as Airbus Industrie's A320 entered service. A true competitor to the 737 in every way, the A320 spurred Boeing to further improve its offering. It introduced the Next Generation (or NG) range of 737 models, namely the 737-600, -700, -800 and -900. The latter was the largest 737 built, capable of carrying up to 215 passengers. The engines used were quieter and more efficient, and the range much improved.

The popularity of these types – in particular the -700 and -800 variants – helped push the success of the 737 even further. By the end of 2009 more than 6,000 737s had been produced.

One of the legacies of the Boeing 737 has been in enabling so-called low-cost airlines to flourish. Whilst Southwest Airlines (largely seen as the originator of the low-cost model) in Texas had initially flown Boeing 727s, it later settled on the 737, which had great reliability, good passenger capacity, could be turned around in thirty minutes, and was cheap to operate. By focusing on this single proven solution, Southwest only had to train pilots for one type of aircraft and could deploy them anywhere across its network. This model was then copied across the world, particularly in Asia and Europe where airlines such as Ryanair opted for the Boeing 737 in huge numbers. To date Southwest Airlines has flown hundreds of 737s across most models, and Ryanair continues to take delivery of numerous -800s per month.

The interior of the modern Boeing 737 MAX. (Author)

Boeing recently launched the 737 MAX variant. (Author)

The cockpit of the 737 MAX offers the latest technology advancements. (Author)

A Boeing 737-200 of Delta Air Lines. (Author's collection)

Ever adaptable, Boeing has continued to invest in and improve its 737 aircraft. The latest variant is the 737 MAX, which entered service in 2017 and shows just as much appeal, with close to 4,000 orders across four main variants standing at the time of writing. It features the new CFM International LEAP engines, a lighter construction and split tip winglet devices to improve aerodynamics. The cockpit is state-of-the-art and, again, three models are on offer to cater for differing capacity needs. With the introduction of the MAX, the 737 is also being touted as a transatlantic airliner that can be used on thinner routes and still turn a profit for airlines, adapting to stand up to competitors around the world proposing and producing rival aircraft.

The Boeing 737 is a true milestone in flight, proving how a design can be continuously adapted over fifty years and always meet the needs of airlines and passengers in all market places.

Southwest Airlines pioneered the low-cost model using Boeing 737s. (Author's collection)

A Boeing 737-500. (Author)

The 737 Next Generation models included the -600, -700 and -800, as seen here. (Author)

The 737 is the most successful jet airliner of all time. From 1967 to its new 737 MAX incarnation, it has taken orders for close to 10,000 aircraft.

On average a Boeing 737 takes off or lands somewhere in the world every five seconds.

Low-cost and holiday companies thrive on the Boeing 737 due to its economics. (Author)

Douglas originally began studying the development of a smaller-range airliner to complement its DC-8 in the 1950s. By the 1960s it had returned to the studies, and created a design for a T-tail airliner with rear-mounted engines to compete with rival aircraft from Boeing and European manufacturers. The resulting sixty-three-seat airliner flew for the first time in 1965, before entering service with Delta Air Lines later the same year.

The specification for the DC-9 was for an aircraft capable of taking off from shorter runways, like the Boeing 727, which was possible given the clean wing since engines were mounted elsewhere. Like the Boeing 737 to come, the DC-9 was also envisaged as an airliner that could be offered in different sizes to satisfy the requirements of different airlines and the routes they fly.

Thus, following the original (and smallest) DC-9-10, later variants included the improved performance -20, the great range -30, and the higher capacity -40 and -50. However, by the time the production run of more than 970 DC-9s came to an end in 1982, the type had already helped establish a new airliner series under what was now McDonnell Douglas.

The MD-80 series was the same basic shape as the DC-9, with a five-abreast seating arrangement, T-tail, short wings and rear-mounted engines. However, the new variant offered significantly more seats and a greater maximum take-off weight.

Swissair became the launch customer for what was officially known as the DC-9 series 80, with the first example entering service in 1981.

The MD-80 offered a number of sub-variants, again to attract as many customers as possible by offering different engine performance characteristics, range and seating capacity. These included the original

MD-81, -82 and -83, followed by the shorter MD-87 and the -88 with improved cockpit.

The DC-9 design would go on to see two more variants, the McDonnell Douglas MD-90 and MD-95. The former is the largest version built, with space for 172 passengers, whilst the latter is more akin to the original DC-9-30. The MD-95 would become the Boeing 717 following the merger of McDonnell Douglas with Boeing in 1997.

All in all, this adaptable aircraft type, which stayed in production across its many variants between 1965 and 2006, has been a true staple of the airline industry. A total of almost 2,500 were built.

An early, shorter Douglas DC-9-15 flying for KLM.
(Author's collection)

The DC-9 entered service with Delta Air Lines in 1965. (Author's collection)

The success of the DC-9 led to many stretched variants, such as this MD-90. (Author's collection)

Following the DC-9, the McDonnell Douglas MD-80 series of aircraft added greater capacity by stretching the fuselage. (Author)

BRITTEN NORMAN BN-2 ISLANDER

Built in some of the most unlikely conditions you could imagine, the Islander has proven to be a durable utility aircraft that is as popular today as it was when production began more than fifty years ago.

Britten-Norman was an engineering firm based on the Isle of Wight, off the south coast of the United Kingdom. Seeing rising demand for small commuter aircraft that were cheap to run, the company developed the twin-engine Islander in 1965, which had an economical, yet strong, design that could carry up to nine passengers with a single crew member and operate from rough, unprepared and short airstrips.

Demand was strong for the Islander, and production began in Romania to supplement the stretched workforce on the Isle of Wight.

A three-engine version known as the Trislander was developed in 1970, and variants have been produced for military operators, too. Other uses include agricultural spraying, as a parachute drop platform, and aerial firefighting.

Today, still in production in Romania, the Islander can be found flying all over the world. It is particularly popular in remoter regions, ferrying passengers around island chains such as the Caribbean, Seychelles and northern Scotland. More than 1,200 examples have been built.

Landing on a beach is just one of the many benefits of the nimble BN-2 Islander. (J.J. Harrison/ Creative Commons)

Concorde wasn't the only supersonic transport aircraft to grace our skies. Developed in parallel to the Anglo/French airliner we're all so familiar with was a rival Soviet supersonic aircraft from Tupolev.

In fact, this particular aircraft resembled Concorde closely and was assumed to be a direct copy. However, it had a few significant differences in how its designers had approached the problem of moving passengers faster than a speeding bullet, including the addition of retractable canards that extended out from either side of the cockpit to increase lift at slow speeds.

The Tu-144 beat Concorde to flight by three months. All effort had been put into making sure it flew before the end of 1968, which was the sixtieth anniversary of the Communist revolution; it managed this on 2 December. The aircraft would also beat Concorde to supersonic flight, passing both Mach 1 and Mach 2 in the first half of 1969. This is a milestone that belongs to the Soviet designers.

However, the haste at which Tupolev was pushed to bring its aircraft to flight left it prone to a number of issues. The Tu-144 was incredibly noisy in the cabin, making it difficult even for passengers sat next to each other to have a conversation.

You may think of Concorde as the first airliner to reach supersonic speeds. However, the Soviet Tu-144 actually beat Concorde to the air and to Mach 1 by several months. Despite this, the aircraft (dubbed 'Concordski') was not a commercial success.

A Tu-144 on display. The type only flew passengers for a short period of time. (Author)

Then, in front of thousands of onlookers, the Tu-144 aircraft being demonstrated at the 1973 Paris Air Show broke up and crashed, significantly harming the reputation of the airliner.

Passenger flights began in November 1977, but ceased only seven months later following regular failures and incidents, and the rising cost of oil. The Tu-144 was relegated to flying mail across the Soviet Union before the project was cancelled in 1983.

Nasa briefly revived one aircraft to use as a flying supersonic testbed in the early 1990s. Despite its failings, the honour of taking a passenger aircraft to supersonic speeds for the first time belongs to the Soviet Union. Its aircraft was better aerodynamically than Concorde, but was inefficient and less reliable.

EMBRAER 110 BANDEIRANTE

In the 1960s, the legendary French aircraft engineer Max Holste was working with the Brazilian government to facilitate the development of a new transport and trainer aircraft for the country's air force. A small, twin-engined turboprop was produced to fit the bill and in order to produce the aircraft, a new company was formed in August 1969 named Embraer.

The new aircraft was named the Bandeirante. Once the air force commitment had been satisfied, Embraer was free to start seeking commercial opportunities for the aircraft. In doing so, the Bandeirante gained some significant orders from around the world.

The type was useful in many roles, from commuter airliners to package freighter and military uses, and came in a number of configurations.

However, the key legacy of this is in establishing what is today one of the world's largest aircraft manufacturing companies. Embraer went on to build the sleeker EMB 120 Brasilia, and then moved into the jet market with the EMB 145, and the larger E-Jet family of aircraft, which have successfully challenged the dominance of the larger Airbus A320 and Boeing 737 families, offering greater capacity and range over earlier Embraer products.

The Bandeirante remained in production until 1990, establishing a reputation from the Brazilian company for well-built, reliable commuter aircraft.

An EMB-110 operating for UK regional carrier Genair.
(Author's collection)

Emerging from the Soviet Union in the early 1960s, the Tupolev Tu-154 was a large T-tail airliner design with three rear-mounted engines. It was similar in style and of a similar era to the Boeing 727 and Hawker Siddeley Trident, which had pioneered the use of three engines at the rear. This design led to a clean wing that allowed greater operating speeds, and the Tu-154 became one of the fastest airliners to fly.

Entering service in 1970, the Tu-154 became a workhorse of the Soviet Union and later Russia, alongside Commonwealth states and countries in Eastern Europe. It did not, however, have any sales success in Western markets, although the type was commonly used to ferry holidaymakers to countries such as Bulgaria even into the 2000s.

Alongside its speed, the Tu-154 offered numerous benefits, including a spacious cabin for up to 180 passengers and a large, sturdy undercarriage that meant the aircraft could safely operate from rough runways often found in the remote regions of Russia. It became a stalwart of airlines such as Russian national carrier Aeroflot, as well as the country's air force, with hundreds of examples flying domestic and European routes. It was only the onset of noise regulations that finally saw Aeroflot retire the type in 2010, although it continues in limited airline service in Russia, and the Russian military is still a major user.

The Tupolev Tu-154 was a large T-tail airliner design with three rear-mounted engines. (Author)

View from the window of a Tu-154 in flight. (Author)

Entering service in 1970, the Tu-154 became a
workhorse of the Soviet Union and Commonwealth
states. (Author)

Concorde is up there as possibly the most famous airliner of all time. Everything about it, from the dart-like shape to its supersonic speeds and on-board luxury, caught the public imagination in a way few other aircraft had. When it was retired, many shed a tear and were unbelieving that this aircraft would no longer grace our skies.

Developed in tandem between the British and French, Concorde emerged at a time when military aircraft development had sped through a period of technological advances following the end of the Second World War. One of the key components developed was the delta-shaped wing, which would become famous on the Vulcan bomber, and this was chosen for the design of Concorde.

A committee had actually been formed in 1956 to develop a supersonic airliner capable of carrying 150 passengers from London to New York at speeds of at least Mach 1.8. The materials required to cope with such speeds and the associated temperatures were difficult to determine and expensive to procure.

As a result, the British sought a partner to help with the design of a supersonic airliner. France had recently developed its own supersonic fighter aircraft, and the Sud Aviation Caravelle airliner was proving a great success. Thus, on 29 November 1962 an agreement was signed between the two countries that would see British Aircraft Corporation and Sud Aviation build the airliner, alongside engine manufacturers Bristol Siddeley (later Rolls-Royce) and SNECMA.

The intricacies that went into the development of Concorde were far beyond all other airliners to date. This aircraft would fly passengers faster and higher than ever before, and undergo stresses and temperatures that would crumple other airliners. Yet, at the opposite end of the spectrum, Concorde was expected to operate from existing airport runways and fit in with the normal air traffic patterns flying at slower speeds as they

The distinctive
arrow-like shape of
Concorde was instantly
recognisable the
world over. (Author's
collection)

approached and departed airports. Concorde featured a unique drooping
nose to give pilots a better view on take-off and landing when the nose
was held high to facilitate flying at slow speeds.

The finalised design settled on a sleek airliner that could typically carry
around 100 passengers at speeds of up to Mach 2, with a range that
comfortably linked cities on either side of the Atlantic. Construction of
the Concorde aircraft would happen simultaneously in factories in Bristol
and Toulouse.

Concorde first flew on 2 March 1969, yet it would not enter airline
service until January 1976. Initial enthusiasm in the aircraft as the future
of travel saw orders and expressions of interest from major airlines
around the world. However, delays in development, the 1973 oil crisis, and
stock market crashes left only two carriers to fly the type – Air France
and British Airways.

The cost of flying Concorde, and the speed advantage it brought passengers, meant it was only ever going to be the preserve of customers who could afford it. This was no surprise, as the development had anticipated that Concorde would be for business and first-class customers.

This, however, helped to elevate the status of Concorde in the eyes of the public, who would look on in awe as it powered into the skies, dreaming of being able to afford the luxury of flying on board. However, utilisation of the fourteen Concordes built for airline service was relatively low and both operator airlines realised that charter work and pleasure flights could be a popular and profitable side venture for their aircraft. As a result, thousands of everyday folk got to experience supersonic flight at a fraction of the cost throughout its operational life.

One of the key selling points of flying Concorde was in allowing businessmen in London or Paris to have breakfast, head to the airport, and travel to New York in time for the start of the working day. It offered a genuine benefit for those who could afford it (or claim it on business expenses), and was a regular haunt of celebrities. Staff specially picked to work on Concorde would know the names of all regular passengers and received special training on how to match the standards associated with the aircraft.

Standard transatlantic flight times were in the region of three and a half hours. Passengers would spend the time sipping Champagne, eating a lavish meal, and enjoying views of the curvature of the earth from 65,000ft.

On 25 July 2000, an unfortunate and catastrophic series of events led to an Air France Concorde crashing in flames shortly after departing Paris Charles de Gaulle Airport. It uncovered severe vulnerabilities in the aircraft design and all aircraft were grounded pending investigation and subsequent modification to protect the fuel tanks from being pierced and igniting, as had happened during the accident.

Concorde returned to service in 2001, but the world of aviation was a different place following the September 11 terrorist attacks in the United States. Both airlines flying the type had found it difficult to make money with their Concorde aircraft, and the diminishing support from Airbus – the successor to the companies that had originally developed it – in the supply of spare parts and technical assistance led to a joint announcement between Air France and British Airways in 2003 that the aircraft would be retired.

Thousands came out to witness the final landings at London Heathrow. All Concorde aircraft were then dispersed to museums around the world and decommissioned, ending a chapter in air travel that had seemed so advanced at the time but would leave no spiritual successor.

Despite its technological advances, only two airlines ever ordered Concorde aircraft. (Author's collection)

It seems the legacy of Concorde will continue to last for many years to come. Children born long after the final flights in 2003 still seem to understand the appeal of the aircraft and marvel at its shape. The association of speed and luxury with Concorde live on in a way not seen with any other aircraft.

Concorde holds the record speed for crossing the Atlantic between Paris and New York in a time of two hours fifty-two minutes. During a typical flight the heating of the airframe would cause it to stretch by up to 10in.

After Concorde, the Boeing 747 'jumbo jet' is probably the most iconic airliner of all time. Most of its fame is a legacy of the hype surrounding its launch, and also from its easily identifiable shape that includes a distinctive lump at the front of the fuselage, where the cockpit and an upstairs seating area were housed.

The story of the 747 began when the United States Air Force put out a request for proposals to build a new military transport aircraft capable of carrying 750 troops anywhere in the world. Boeing put a lot of effort into the design, for nothing of this scale had been seen before. The project would be awarded to Lockheed, which produced the C-5 Galaxy transport aircraft, however, Boeing recognised its research could still be used to develop a new high-capacity passenger aircraft. As had happened previously with the 707, Boeing reached a point where it was literally betting the company on this new aircraft, and thankfully it was a gamble that paid off.

The company courted Pan American Airways – at the time the largest airline in the United States, with a global reach. In consultation with the airline's infamous leader, Juan Trippe, many iterations were considered, including double hulls, double decks and different configurations of wings, engines and tail layout.

One of the biggest problems to overcome was in how to safely accommodate and also evacuate such a high number of passengers, and how to power such a huge machine. Boeing had settled on seven candidate designs for the 747 and built mock-up cabins for Trippe to inspect in March 1966.

Pan Am's chief engineer disliked many of the designs and had a final say in the layout. Because Boeing's team had been designing the 747 from the outset as a cargo aircraft that could also be used for passengers, it was felt that a wide fuselage was necessary that could carry standard

Pan American was instrumental in the development and design of the Boeing 747. It operated the first flight of the type in January 1970. (Jon Proctor)

The elevated cockpit of the Boeing 747. (Author)

light containers on its main deck. However, the question arose as to how to load such a cargo. It was decided therefore to raise the cockpit above the main deck of the aircraft, allowing cargo to be loaded straight in by lifting the nose. This resulted in the famous hump at the front of the 747.

Trippe liked the idea of the upper deck, as he felt passenger staterooms or a lounge could be fitted in the passenger variant of the aircraft. He insisted on windows being added to the upper deck for that reason.

Another first introduced by the 747 would be a twin-aisle cabin, with typically nine- or ten-abreast seating for passengers. Prior to this airliners had always been single aisle.

A unique aspect of the Boeing 747 was its spiral staircase leading to the upper deck and cockpit above the main cabin. (Author)

The 747 is still in production as the -800 model, but few airlines have ordered it. (Author)

An order was placed by Pan Am on 12 April 1966 for twenty-five aircraft at a cost of $18,757,000 each – a total order of $500 million when engines and parts were included.

The scale of the Boeing 747 was so huge that it necessitated a new way of building aircraft. A giant new production building was erected at Paine Field near Seattle; today this building is the largest in the world by area. When the time came for the first flight of the behemoth aircraft on Sunday, 9 February 1969, the president of Boeing, Bill Allen, told test pilot Jack Waddell: 'Jack, I hope you understand the future of the company rides with you guys this morning.' Such an investment had been made by Boeing that it could not afford the project to fail.

Although Pan Am, and a number of other airlines, had made an incredible commitment to the 747 by ordering it off the design board, if it ultimately proved to be a failure the compensation and cost of the investment to date would cripple the company.

However, Allen need not have worried as the prototype, N7470, lifted gracefully into the skies and Waddell was able to demonstrate its surprisingly light controls with some playful manoeuvres in the skies over the assembled crowds.

The 747 went on to serve with hundreds of airlines in huge numbers. Later variants were added that each improved performance and passenger capacity, increasing the length of the hump, and adding winglets for better fuel efficiency. There was even a short SP, or Special Performance, version that held fewer passengers but travelled much farther than any other airliner at the time.

A key success factor of the 747, which was realised early on by Pan Am, was in its passenger economies. By carrying up to 550 passengers at once, the cost of travel was greatly reduced. Combined with its range, which

The cockpit of one of the early Boeing 747 models. (Author)

KLM is one of the airlines still flying the popular 747-400 on scheduled services. (Author)

A Virgin Atlantic Boeing 747-400. (Author)

The 747 had the nickname 'jumbo jet'. It has been in continuous production since 1969, and six different main versions have been produced. It was also chosen as the platform for Air Force One, which carries the US President.

The tail of the 747 stands 63ft (19m) tall – equivalent to a six-storey building.

could easily cross the Atlantic or Pacific oceans, this aircraft contributed single-handedly to bringing long distance travel to the masses.

In 2016 Boeing celebrated the remarkable fiftieth anniversary of the 747. Undoubtedly in decline today, it has enjoyed incredible success and became the benchmark for large passenger transport aircraft. The jumbo could be seen all over the world, and was even popular on short domestic routes in countries such as Japan, where large numbers of passengers commute by air.

The latest model, the 747-8, is still in production, but demand has been poor and the production rate has reduced. It has introduced many of the advances in composite construction and on-board systems seen in the 787 Dreamliner, and was seen as an answer to the rival Airbus A380. However, most examples produced are for use as freighters, and with older models being retired by airlines as they advance in age the chance to fly on a jumbo jet may sadly be in its final chapter.

Whether any future aircraft will be as iconic as the 747 (often dubbed the 'queen of the skies') remains to be seen. It was the world's first wide-body airliner and introduced new levels of comfort not seen since the golden age of the flying boats. It then successfully transitioned into an efficient transporter of huge numbers of passengers when luxury became less important to the airlines. Returning full circle, it was also a highly efficient freighter aircraft capable of carrying outsized loads over long distances.

When the final passenger flight by a McDonnell Douglas DC-10 took place in 2014, some commentators called time on what was considered to be a troublesome aircraft with a tarnished history. A series of fatal crashes early in its career gave the large three-engine jet a bad name, particularly when each disaster resulted in hundreds of deaths and were caused by mechanical issues.

However, other commentators at the time of the final flights lamented the DC-10's passing, labelling it a workhorse and one of the jets that truly shaped the way we travel today.

Developed as an answer to Boeing's early dominance in the widebody market with its 747, and alongside Lockheed's similar L-1011 TriStar, the DC-10 was a large, powerful machine capable of carrying well over 300 people and travelling great distances. Introduced in 1971, many of the world's great airlines operated the type, using it to open routes to new markets; it was also common on domestic flights within the United States, and used in the early days of low-cost travel by the likes of British aviation pioneer Freddie Laker.

Like so many aircraft types of its era, as more fuel efficient and cost effective aircraft were introduced the venerable DC-10 was slowly replaced, finding a new role as a cargo freighter.

In addition to the 377 passenger DC-10s built, the type was also used extensively by the US Air Force as an air-to-air refuelling tanker known as the KC-10. In 1991, the stretched MD-11 was also unveiled, which could carry more passengers over greater distances. Only 200 examples were built, however, as twin-engine airliners started to offer cost savings over the same distances that the MD-11 offered.

Developed as a rival to the dominance of the Boeing 747 and Lockheed TriStar, the DC-10 was a popular large airliner. (Jon Proctor)

A Japan Air Lines DC-10 in Mumbai. (Jimmy Wadia)

Pan Am, unusually, only flew DC-10s for a short time. (Author's collection)

Europe has always had a strong heritage of building aircraft, particularly in countries such as France, Germany, Italy, Netherlands, Spain and the United Kingdom. Within each of these, aircraft and engine manufacturers had consistently collaborated and merged operations, and international boundaries were crossed when the British Aircraft Corporation and Aérospatiale joined forces to create the Anglo–French Concorde aircraft. Around the same time as Concorde, proposals were under way to develop a new aircraft to compete against the dominance of US manufacturers Boeing, Lockheed and McDonnell Douglas. It was to be a collaboration between different companies, and would lead to the formation of Airbus Industrie in 1967 – an organisation owned by Aérospatiale, Deutsche Airbus, Hawker Siddeley and Fokker-VFW. Later, Spanish company CASA would also acquire a share.

Just as with Concorde, parts for the Airbus aircraft would be produced remotely by the various manufacturers and shipped to assembly locations in France and Germany.

The A300 was the first aircraft produced by Airbus, which is today one of the two largest airliner manufacturers in the world. This new aircraft was also the first wide-body airliner to only have two engines.

The most unusual variant of the A300 is the Beluga, which is used by Airbus to transport aircraft parts between its factories. (Author)

Airbus A300B4 cabin interior. (Author)

Orion Airways operated Airbus A300s to ferry holidaymakers to Mediterranean destinations in the 1980s. (Author's collection)

The final operator of passenger A300s in the UK was Monarch Airlines. (Author)

The new aircraft was soon named the A300, representing its target capacity of 300 to 320 passengers. Using a clean sheet with no legacy designs enabled Airbus to target state-of-the-art technology when designing the A300, aiming to harness feedback from airlines over what features and specifications they would seek in a new aircraft.

The result would be the world's first passenger aircraft to use composite materials in its construction, and the first twin-engine aircraft to feature a wide-body cabin (one with two aisles).

The Airbus A300 first flew on 28 October 1972 and entered service with Air France in 1974. It would produce the smaller A310 derivative, and the updated A300-600 that would feature fly-by-wire technology and offer adaptability to allow airlines to just as easily fly the aircraft on short-haul trunk routes as long-distance premium services. It would also become a popular freighter aircraft for cargo airlines.

The A300 established Airbus as a major aircraft manufacturer and revitalised European aircraft production for the coming decades.

An Airbus A310, which was developed from the larger A300. (Author)

50 AIRLINERS THAT CHANGED FLYING

Originally launched in 1971 as the natural progression from the de Havilland Comet and Hawker Siddeley Trident, the HS.146 did not see the light of day until Britain's three main aircraft manufacturing companies were merged to form British Aerospace.

When work continued in 1978, the BAe 146 emerged as a new generation of regional jet that was set to revolutionise air travel. First off, the small airliner was incredibly quiet compared to earlier generation airliners, gaining it the nickname 'Whisperjet'. Secondly, it was designed with short runways in mind, enabling carriers to use it as a commuter into smaller city airports while not suffering a penalty in the number of passengers carried or range available. Its low noise emissions helped with city centre operations, such as those at London City.

The BAe 146 featured a high wing with four small jet engines mounted underneath. It came in three passenger variants, seating between 70 and 100 passengers, while a package freighter version was popular with cargo companies, and the British government even used the type to transport the royal family.

In the 1990s the BAe 146 was revitalised, with three new variants (each roughly similar in size to the original models) now under the Avro banner. These were the RJ70, RJ85 and RJ100 respectively (RJ was short for Regional Jet). Each featured uprated engines and new cockpits, among other improvements, and helped cement the popularity of the family of airliners. They would go on to become the best-selling British jet ever produced. Production ceased in 2001 when airlines moved to aircraft with fewer engines.

Left: An Avro RJ85, developed as an upgraded BAe 146. (Author)

Below left: Many British operators chose the 146 to operate scheduled services. (Author's collection)

Below right: The British Aerospace 146 features four quiet engines slung from a high wing. (Author)

By the late 1970s, Boeing had found itself trailing its new rival, Airbus, for the first time. The European manufacturer had seen a good start with its new A300 and A310 models, which were the first twin-aisle (widebody) airliners to use only two engines.

Boeing's own answer to this was the 767, which is a similar configuration, offering a twin-aisle cabin capable of seating 290 passengers. Its range made the aircraft suitable for longer trips of 3,900 miles (7,200km), with an 'extended range' version soon offered that stretched this to 6,590 miles (12,200km).

Unlike all of Boeing's previous aircraft, the 767 was one of the first airliners to be developed with an electronic flight instrument system (EFIS) built into the cockpit as standard. This introduced cathode ray tube screens to display information about the aircraft's systems where previously only clockwork dials were used.

Much of the 767's early success when introduced in 1981 (particularly before the extended range version was built) was with the so-called legacy airlines in the United States, including Delta Air Lines and United Airlines, who used the aircraft on the busy trunk routes between the

Britannia Airways flew
Boeing 767s on holiday
charter flights. (Author)

The 767 has proven popular for transatlantic routes, including those of American Airlines. (Author)

east and west coasts. However, airlines around the world soon realised the 767's potential, including leisure airlines such as Britannia Airways in the UK that could use the high capacity to ferry holidaymakers around Europe in large numbers.

The 767 was stretched in 1983, adding an extra 10ft (3m) of fuselage to enable it to carry extra passengers. This, the 767-300, was the most popular variant and became particularly common on transatlantic flights in the 1990s, as well as with airlines across the Far East.

Looking for a follow-up to its successful 727 airliner, Boeing had also designed the narrow body twin-jet 757 at a similar time to the 767. Both aircraft featured a common cockpit, meaning crews could fly either aircraft on the same licence. As such, a number of airlines ordered both aircraft types for their fleets.

50 AIRLINERS THAT CHANGED FLYING

This small utility aircraft, developed by one of the world's most successful light aircraft manufacturers, is still in production today, thirty-five years since its first flight.

The Cessna 208 was developed with a wide range of uses in mind, and a design that could facilitate any kind of flying, from unprepared airstrips in wild and remote locations, to regular airline operations seating up to fourteen passengers in comfort. Its interior can easily be switched from seats to open space, and the reliable engine and need for only one pilot makes it an affordable option.

As such, this aircraft has seen more than 2,500 examples built and can be found in nearly every country on earth. It is particularly common in supporting relief, missionary and tourism operators in Africa and Asia, and as a package carrier in North America. It is also common to see the 208 used as a parachute jump platform, or supporting military organisations.

The success of the Caravan is down to the many different uses it has, from carrying passengers and cargo; to parachuting; firefighting; border patrol; carrying troops and military supplies; supporting mission organisations in developing countries and even spraying crops and pollution.

The Cessna Caravan utility aircraft has been in
production for more than thirty-five years.
(Public domain)

When Airbus started development of its new short- to medium-haul airliner in the early 1980s, it had its sights firmly set on challenging the dominance of the Boeing 737 in this market. At this time Airbus only had two aircraft in its stable, the wide-bodies A300 and A310, which had pioneered the early use of fly-by-wire technology.

With confidence in their new aircraft plans shown by Air France in 1981, Airbus pressed ahead and officially launched the A320 in 1984. It would take the idea of fly-by-wire much further and redefine the airliner cockpit beyond anything seen before. The classic control column in front of pilots was replaced by a side stick much like a computer joystick. This would send electric signals to key control surfaces around the aircraft, which would then interpret the signals into movement. The many dials and instruments seen in cockpits thus far were also replaced in the A320 by digital screens that could show key information to pilots at the touch of a button.

An Airbus A320, one of the most successful airliners of all time. (Author)

Above left: Airbus developed the A320 to counter the dominance of the Boeing 737. (Author)

Above right: The smaller Airbus A319. (Author)

The cockpit innovations in the A320 would become standard in most future airliners from all manufacturers as the age of the 'glass cockpit' developed through the 1980s and '90s. However, with the A320, Airbus developed the idea of using a standard cockpit layout that would transfer across all aircraft types it built. So, for example, a pilot trained to operate the A320 would feel at home in the A330 or even the A380 super jumbo, and would be able to fly them with minimal training compared to the transition times pilots experienced between the Boeing 737 and 777.

By the time the first Airbus A320 flew on 22 February 1987, Boeing's 737 had twenty years' head start. However, the timing was perfect, and major airlines supporting Airbus' efforts with significant early orders.

Like the Boeing 737, Airbus had planned early in the A320 development to introduce different-sized variants to better cover the needs of airlines. The first of these was the stretched A321, launched in 1988 with space for an additional thirty to forty passengers. Similarly, the shorter A319 was launched in 1992 and typically carryied 134 passengers. Finally, in 1999, the even shorter 107-seat A318 was launched. This gave Airbus the ability to greater match the variants on offer by Boeing's 737, as well as its 757 and the smaller regional jets being produced by Bombardier and Embraer. However, with pilots able to switch between types easily, airlines could reduce the training costs associated with operating aircraft from different manufacturers.

The A320 has undoubtedly been an amazing success for Airbus, growing to contend the success of its rival Boeing 737 in orders. Anyone flying today has a strong chance of flying one of the A320 family aircraft, with close to 8,000 having been built at the time of writing.

As aircraft technology has advanced, Airbus launched the A320neo (new engine option) in 2010, making its first flight in 2014, followed by the A321neo and A319neo. These models offer efficiency and aerodynamic improvements, a more spacious cabin, and new, more fuel-efficient engines.

A stretched Airbus A321 variant operating for Thomas Cook Airlines. (Author)

Despite the sales success of the 727 and 737, the sheer brilliance of the 747, and the technological advances of the 787 Dreamliner, the 777 is regarded by many as the best aircraft Boeing has ever built.

During the early 1990s it was clear airlines needed to save money on long-haul flying. The 1980s-era Boeing 757 and 767 were well received, but built with earlier technology. Likewise, the 747 was popular with passengers, but was better suited to higher-capacity routes. With competition coming from Airbus in the form of the A330 and A340, Boeing created the 777 – one of its most successful aircraft to date.

Older generation aircraft at the time, such as the Lockheed TriStar and Douglas DC-10, were reaching the end of their life, making Boeing's timing perfect with the introduction of the 'Triple Seven'. For the first time the company developed an aircraft entirely using computer-aided design and set its sights on creating its first fly-by-wire aircraft, something Airbus had been championing for a number of years.

Most major airlines around the world use Boeing 777s for long-haul services. (Author)

The stretched 777-300, which typically carries up to 396 passengers. (Author)

Each of the two engines on the 777 have the largest diameter of any airliner, with the equivalent cross section as that of the Boeing 737 cabin, at 13ft (4m) wide. The 777 was Boeing's first fly-by-wire aircraft, and was the world's first airliner to be designed entirely by computer.

Passengers on board the 777 would experience much more comfort and space than the likes of the 767. It could seat up to 313 passengers in a two-class layout and featured two engines with the largest diameter ever seen on an aircraft. These engines were produced by Pratt & Whitney, Rolls Royce and General Electric and featured a huge output of power, yet were quieter than previous aircraft.

The 777 was so successful that stretched and long-range variants soon followed. Today they are flown in huge numbers by most of the world's major airlines, particularly in the Middle East and Asia, where the capacity and range give great flexibility on the routes flown.

With the introduction of the 747 in 1969, Boeing had continuously flown the flag for large passenger aircraft that had never been surpassed in size or capacity, even by rivals McDonnell Douglas and Lockheed. However, the European Airbus consortium had repeatedly targeted the products on offer from rivals – in particular Boeing – by producing its own aircraft to match or replace existing aircraft, and since the late 1980s had been exploring the possibility of a high-capacity airliner to compete with the 747 'jumbo jet'.

Designated the A3XX, work officially began in 1994, covering a variety of layout designs and options. It quickly settled on a double-deck configuration running the length of the fuselage, rather than the hump at the front of the 747, and harking back to the early flying boats of the 1930s and '40s.

Airbus was quick to get the public on board with its new aircraft, long before it even took to the skies. Clever marketing showed off the possibilities of incorporating gyms, restaurants, shopping arcades and lounges in the spacious interior. However, the economic background at the time was of financial crisis in world markets and Airbus knew that it had to compete on costs and allow customer airlines to make significant savings per seat over the rival 747.

The resulting aircraft was a mammoth in every sense. It targeted point-to-point services between the world's large hub airports, allowing airlines to transport up to a proposed 868 passengers in the highest capacity layout.

The design featured four large turbofan engines slung under wings that had a span of almost 260ft (80m). The interior uses two staircases – one forward and one at the rear – whilst the spacious cockpit for two crew members sits in a mid-position between the two floors and utilises the latest in avionics technology. For the first time pilots made use of a

paperless cockpit, designed to reduce the clutter of manuals and charts, replacing them with touch screens and intuitive interfaces.

Yet, despite its size and complexity, the A380's cockpit was designed to mirror those of other Airbus aircraft so that pilots could quickly transition to it with minimal training.

Initial orders came in for the A380 from airlines in Asia, Europe and the Middle East in particular. Given warning of its impending arrival, airports around the world rushed to make adjustments to their runways, taxiways and passenger loading jetways, for no aircraft of this size had ever been handled regularly before. Being 'A380 ready' became the buzz phrase as airports prepared for the huge aircraft and the hundreds of extra passengers it would bring on every flight.

When the Airbus A380 first flew in 2003 it was an event broadcast on TV news channels around the world. Public hype around the aircraft,

Above left: Emirates is the world's largest operator of Airbus A380 'super jumbos'. (Author)

Above right: The A380 has proven popular with Middle Eastern airlines, who offer on-board luxuries such as suites and showers. (Author)

The A380 has the largest passenger capacity of any airliner. (Author)

The A380 has 40 per cent more useable space than a Boeing 747, and can carry a maximum of 875 passengers at once! Despite its size and four huge engines, it is one of the quietest airliners you can fly.

which is the largest passenger aircraft ever to fly, had grown to a level of excitement not seen since the 747 and Concorde.

Since its introduction, passengers lucky enough to travel on an A380 have gushed about how quiet and comfortable it is. The gyms and shops have not materialised, yet some airlines have introduced such features as on-board showers and private suites to attract high-yield customers.

A little over 200 aircraft had been built at the time of writing, with orders slowing to a trickle. It seems the A380 will always be somewhat of a niche aircraft, but it has proven the possibilities of very large aircraft when the right materials, powerplants and technology are available.

In the 1990s Boeing began looking at its next generation of aircraft to build on the successes it had seen with the previous generation. The Seattle-based manufacturer started proposing a larger variant of the 747, and also a smaller 'Sonic Cruiser' airliner that could travel much faster for the same costs as its current offerings.

However, following the 11 September 2001 terrorist attacks and the subsequent global slump in airline travel and increase in fuel costs, Boeing recognised that it must follow a different path towards its next product.

The 787 was born out of the early designs for the Sonic Cruiser, but was instead of a similar size to the 767 and aimed at offering efficiency, long range and technological advances to improve performance and passenger comfort. It was launched in 2003, and named 'Dreamliner' following a public competition.

Early designs for the 787 were a little more outlandish, but the finished result, rolled out behind schedule in 2007, was of a more traditional design. Many of the features, such as the nose and cockpit shape, and the distinctive upward bend of the wings, give the Dreamliner a very modern appeal.

The 787 was the first airliner to be made mostly of composite materials in its fuselage, wings and tail. These are carbon fibre-reinforced polymer, which offers great strength, yet at a fraction of the weight of the usual aluminium material. The reduced weight meant more fuel and payload could be carried.

The Dreamliner offered a huge advantage for airlines that had been well marketed, and more than 670 orders had been placed by the time the prototype appeared, breaking all records for a new airliner. The advantages included its superior range – the 787 can fly up to 8,786 miles (14,140km) – and the lower seat-per-mile costs than many of its

Above left: An Air Canada Dreamliner on approach to London Heathrow. (Author)

Above right: The 787 comes in three variants. Here a -9 model of Air France. (Author)

rivals, meaning airlines could open up new long-distance routes without needing A380 or 747 passenger payloads to recoup the costs.

For passengers, the cabin had been designed to offer a more spacious feel, with mood lighting and a redesigned window system where blinds were no longer used. Instead, buttons could darken or lighten the window to suit the passenger. For long flights, the Dreamliner claims to leave passengers feeling fresher, with fewer effects of jet lag thanks to the aircraft being pressurised to a lower density altitude, with a much higher humidity. This is possible thanks to the composite materials used, which do not suffer the same levels of fatigue as aluminium from the cabin pressurisation process.

Finally, the cockpit was also revolutionised, offering a futuristic space for pilots to work. Built with the idea of removing the need for paper in mind, displays offer all information on large LCD screens, with a head-up display (HUD) to show important information as pilots look ahead out of the windows. The entire aircraft is fly-by-wire, and pilots who already fly the Boeing 777 can easily convert to the 787, saving training costs.

Boeing offers three variants of the Dreamliner, each a different length and with different ranges and passenger capacities. More than 1,250 orders had been received by the end of 2017, making it one of the most successful widebody airliners ever built. Airbus followed Boeing's example in 2013 with the A350, which is based on similar principles of lightweight composite materials, quieter and more powerful engines, and the ability to fly long distances. It too has sold well.

Below left: The name 'Dreamliner' was chosen in a public competition. (Author)

Below right: The prototype Dreamliner displays the logos of airlines that ordered the type. (Author)

The 787 has removed the need for window shades; instead passengers can darken or lighten their window at the touch of a button. (Author)

It is said that flying on the Dreamliner will make you less jet-lagged than any other aircraft. This is because the cabin is pressurised to a lower altitude, providing more oxygen for passengers on long flights.

It can also easily handle the longest non-stop passenger flights ever flown, such as London to Perth or Abu Dhabi to Auckland. We've come a long way from the 120ft journey of the Wright Brothers.